BARNES & NOBLE BASICS™

getting a
grant

by Barbara Loos

BARNES
&NOBLE
BOOKS

Titles in the **Barnes & Noble Basics**™ series:
Barnes & Noble Basics *Volunteering*

introduction

Alison had some writing experience, so it was only natural that she was asked to write a grant proposal for her local library. "I love my hometown, and our library is a big part of it. They desperately needed funding for a new children's wing, and I was more than willing to try to get a grant. Well, I started to research the process for applying for one, and soon I was spending hours online. Turns out that each foundation has its own specific guidelines on how to apply for a grant! Who knew the nonprofit world was so big and unwieldy?"

Who indeed? Enter **Barnes & Noble Basics** *Getting a Grant*. It not only explains how the nonprofit world works, it also shows you how to successfully navigate through that world to find grant dollars. All you need to know is here: How to define your project, research donors, write a grant proposal, create a budget, customize your proposal, and much more. Read on and get the inside scoop on the ways of nonprofit funding. Your grant money is out there—and getting it just became a whole lot easier.

Barb Chintz
Editorial Director, the **Barnes & Noble Basics**™ series

table of contents

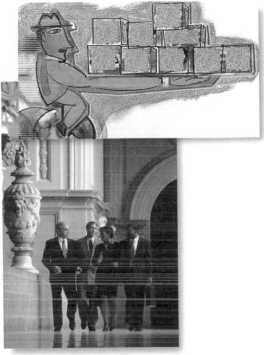

Getting started

what is a grant?

Money for a cause

A **grant** is money given to a worthy cause. A worthy cause, like beauty, is in the eye of the beholder, but getting a grant for a project usually requires that the result will have real social value—such as starting an AIDS resource center, sending an underprivileged honor student to college, or beautifying your hometown. Grants are awarded for all sorts of things. So if you have a worthy cause in mind—or you know of a charity that needs financial help to start a project—you should be considering a grant.

Who gives out grants? **Donors** (also known as **grantmakers**). They are a diverse group, ranging from big philanthropic institutions such as the Rockefeller Foundation to federal, state, and local governments, from small foundations to concerned wealthy individuals. But whether well-known or obscure, wealthy or moderately funded, donors have money earmarked for worthy causes. And many have a powerful motivation to give: The IRS penalizes private foundations that do not give away a minimum of 5% of their investment assets.

To first-time grant seekers, this may seem like a dream come true. You've got a great idea, and they have the money. All you need is to bring the two together. And that's where you'll need the techniques described in this book, because the grant world can be difficult to navigate. Each donor has its own way of doing things, and to win a grant you must learn what each donor expects from you. This can take time and patience, but it can be done if you take it one step at a time. Read on and you'll see how.

SK THE EXPERTS

How many donors are there?

There are approximately 56,000 private foundations in the U.S. In 2002 they gave away a total of $29 billion in grants. And that's not counting agencies in federal and state government, which also have funds in the budget for donating as grants. It's a huge world.

I am confused. Is there a difference between getting a grant and fund-raising?

Yes. A grant is usually a one-time allocation of money. **Fund-raising** is the ongoing process of raising money, including, for example, a membership drive, charity balls to fund the hospital pediatrics wing, car washes for school athletic equipment, or a campaign to ask wealthy individuals for significant contributions. Getting a grant is just one vital part of fund-raising.

As the number of foundations has steadily grown, charitable giving has risen significantly.

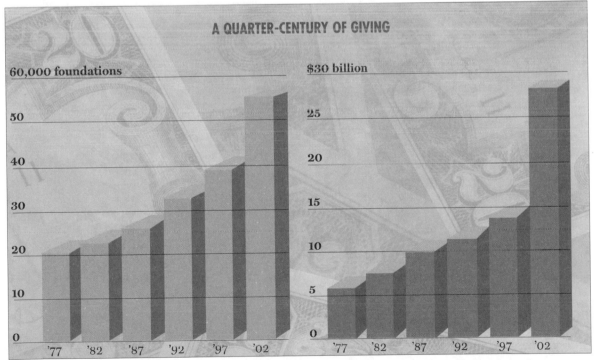

Source: The Foundation Center

what are grants for?

Funds for all sorts of needs

The job of the donor is to provide support (by way of grant money) when needs arise. Alas, donors are not sugar daddies: They can't fund everything. So what kinds of needs do they like to fund? They fall into the following categories.

- Funding a new project
- Meeting an emergency need
- Supporting an ongoing need

Most donors prefer to fund new projects. It's exciting to provide the **seed money** (money that launches a new project) for a cause that will make the world a better place. Ideally, once this project is up and running, it will be self-sustaining—meaning it will get its money from fund-raising activities and not from grants. For example, a project to tutor underperforming readers calls for training volunteers (hence the need for grant money). Once the volunteers are trained, the project carries on by itself. In an ideal grant-making world, funded projects require only a one-time or short-term commitment of grant money. Small wonder funders like these so much. (This book is intended mostly for those seeking grants to fund such projects.)

But funders also understand the need for money in emergencies, such as a new boiler for your town library or a van for a Meals on Wheels organization to replace the one that got totaled in an accident. Most organizations try to have reserve funds or endowments to cover such emergencies, but sometimes it's not enough. Enter the need for grant money.

Some donors will also help support projects on an ongoing basis. Those types of grants are usually reserved for the arts or for ongoing social issues such as homelessness or hunger.

When the Donor Has an Idea

Think about it: If you were in the business of giving away money for worthy causes, chances are you would get pretty good at spotting future needs and causes. Why wait for other people to address those needs? Why not be proactive, identify the need, and ask for grant proposals to fund? That's exactly what government agencies and some foundations do when they make a **Request for Proposals** (RFP), **Request for Applications**, or a **Broad Agency Announcement** (BAA). For instance, after the 9/11 attacks there were a number of RFP's for projects supporting homeland security.

Announcements for RFP's, RFA's, and BAA's are made in various philanthropic newsletters and magazines, and you can also find them online at various sites. For example, the Web site for the Foundation Center (**www.fdncenter.org**), keeps a listing of recent RFP's by private foundations. In these announcements, the funder sometimes offers meetings or workshops to help grant writers understand what kind of program the funder has in mind. If you think there's a fit between their program and yours, then by all means attend. Going to these meetings or workshops is crucial because it gives you the inside track on what the donor is thinking, not to mention the opportunity to meet someone from the donor's organization. Face-to-face meetings are a great way to counteract the faceless paper-to-paper aspect of grant writing.

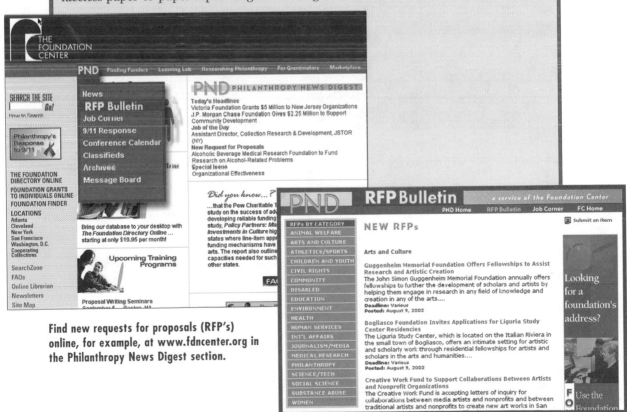

Find new requests for proposals (RFP's) online, for example, at www.fdncenter.org in the Philanthropy News Digest section.

what's your project?

How to start thinking like a funder

The first step in getting together a grant proposal is to describe clearly why you need a grant. The donors have funds to give and a clear idea of the kinds of projects they want to fund. They are motivated to give funds, but they need to match their money with the "right" causes.

Your task is to teach the donors about your project. Before you do anything else you need to work out the basics of your project. These are the key questions to which donors will want answers.

- **What is the project?** Describe what you are trying to do and why.

- **Who will benefit?** What demographic groups do you want to help? You'll have to break down the gender, age, race, and geographic locality of the people your project will help.

- **How will it help?** Explain exactly how this project will make a difference.

- **How much money will the project need?** Basically, you will have to create a budget. It can be hard to figure out how much funding you need. You want to include **direct costs**, such as the price of books for a reading program, but also **indirect costs**, such as expenses for a volunteer appreciation party.

- **Who will help to implement the project?** Do you have a staff on hand? Do you need to create one?

- **When do you need the money?** Handle this question with care because foundations have their own budget cycles, and they may not match your needs perfectly. It pays to plan ahead!

- **How will you evaluate the success of your project?** Do you have a way to objectively measure its success?

ASK THE EXPERTS

My project is pretty simple, but getting a grant sounds really complicated. Are all these steps really necessary?

This process isn't really that complicated. It calls for you to describe your project accurately—something you or some other members of your nonprofit organization should be able to do. And because your project is simple it will be much easier to describe it and create a budget. Remember: When you're seeking funds, think like a funder. Grants go to the cause the donor likes the best—and the donor will only be able to judge that with solid information. Consider these planning steps as tools to help you get what you want.

How long will I have to wait for a decision about whether I get a grant?

That depends on the foundation's **grant cycle** (when the foundation's board of directors meets to vote on grants). Expect the process to take several months from the grant proposal's due date. You can often find the decision date in the grant application guidelines. But if the date is not listed anywhere, there is nothing wrong with asking the foundation's program officer how long the decision-making process will take.

What's the hardest part about getting a grant?

Finding the right donor. Contrary to popular opinion, writing the grant is not the most time-consuming task. The search for the right donor demands more time and attention. The more you do up front to identify the right donor, the better your chances of getting a grant. The number one reason grants are rejected is because they are sent to inappropriate donors. That's why it's smart to focus a lot of attention on finding the right donors.

grants and taxes

How worthy causes get a tax break

Grant money must be given or funneled through a nonprofit organization, such as a school or charity. Why? It's a tax thing. **Nonprofits** by definition are not in the business of making money solely for the enrichment of their workers or shareholders. Because of that, the IRS gives them a federal tax exemption on the money they get from fund-raising and grants. Moreover, people and foundations that give money to nonprofits can deduct their contributions from their taxes, too. It's a win-win situation for good causes.

For most grants, the nonprofit rule is purely academic. Chances are you are writing a grant proposal for just such a nonprofit to begin with. However, if you are seeking a grant for a project that is not affiliated with a nonprofit, you need to get a **nonprofit sponsor,** such as a school or a nonprofit charity. Remember: Only nonprofits can receive grant money. (Read more on how to find a nonprofit sponsor in chapter 2.) There is one exception: If you are applying for grant money for yourself as an individual (see chapter 7), you do not need a nonprofit sponsor.

Community Center

NON-PROFIT ORG
U.S. POSTAGE
P A I D
PERMIT NO. 125
KATONAH, NY

84 Bedford Road • Katonah, NY 10536
Tel: (914) 232-6572 • Fax (914) 232-6574
email: commctr@bestweb.net
www.katonahny.com/CommunityCenter.html

ASK THE EXPERTS

How does an organization become a nonprofit?

To gain nonprofit status, an organization must file for incorporation as a nonprofit in the same state as its headquarters. This involves preparing a legal document that lists the name of the nonprofit and the nature of its work, gives the names and addresses of its board of directors, and lists the group's bylaws. The IRS then reviews the paperwork, and if everything checks out, the tax authorities issue the nonprofit its all-important 501(c)3 tax exemption and a tax ID number. Nonprofits do not have to pay federal income tax on money they earn from fundraising or grant money they receive. They also get a break on postage.

When I apply for a grant, how does the donor know if I have a nonprofit sponsor or not?

One of the first things a donor looks for is a copy of your nonprofit sponsor's 501(c)3 letter from the IRS. You must include this documentation in your grant proposal. (Once again, you do not need to worry about this if you are seeking a grant for yourself as an individual; see chapter 7.)

I am writing a grant proposal for my town. Do I need a nonprofit sponsor?

You already have one! States, cities, towns, and villages are considered nonprofit organizations under tax law.

Are all grant donors nonprofits too?

For the most part, yes. Foundations that give out money for grants are all nonprofit. Again, it's a tax thing. In fact, some of these nonprofit foundations were created by corporations or wealthy individuals to formalize their gift-giving—and qualify for that much-desired tax break.

the grant process

Grants in a nutshell

Once you've got the basics of your project mapped out, you are ready to start considering donors. There is no shortage of grant-makers out there—tens of thousands of them fund all sorts of projects. Your goal is to find the right match between your project and a donor—or even several donors. You will use the Internet and other sources to help you search (more about that in chapters 5 and 6).

Once you have identified a shortlist of likely donors, determine how they want to be approached. Different grantmakers require different approaches. Some donors want extremely detailed information, while others want it short and to the point. Some  want a full-blown **grant proposal**—a package of paperwork that includes a cover letter, a budget, and detailed information on how the project will be executed and evaluated. Some donors want you to write a **letter of intent**—a minisummary of your project and your funding needs—before they will even consider looking at a full proposal. And still others want you to answer their questions using their **application form** to organize the information in an easy-to-process format. Some even let you do this using e-mail.

What's a first-time grant writer to do? Relax and take a deep breath. Fortunately, most donors do provide quite specific **grant-writing guidelines** to help you write a proposal that suits their needs. The good news is that many donors now have Web sites detailing these guidelines and specific instructions about how to approach them in a quest for grant money. They will tell you if you need only submit a letter of intent—or a grant proposal with 16 photocopies.

SK THE EXPERTS

How do I know which donors are right to fund my project?

Research. Your goal is to find a donor whose interests and mission match the goals of your project. Happily, the Internet has made finding that information fairly easy. (Read more about this on page 86.)

Can't I just call up a foundation and ask them how to go about getting a grant?

That's not a good use of anyone's time, especially if the information is available on the funder's Web site. Before cold-calling a grant maker, do a little leg work. If there is no specific information on a funder's Web site (or if there's no Web site), then feel free to call and ask. But don't make this your first step. (For more on calling a donor, see page 140).

FIRST PERSON DISASTER STORY
Play by the Rules

I was new to grantwriting and didn't quite believe that all the rules and regulations really mattered. It was the quality of the project that was important, not whether I filled out an application form. Right? Wrong. I found three ideal funders, all of whom requested that an application form be filled out. I decided to skip it and just send in my proposal. Much to my surprise, I got a letter from each one. One rejected the proposal outright for not having the application form. The other two said I needed to reapply with the proper form before they could consider our project. It doesn't matter how worthwhile your project is or how urgent your need, you've got to follow the rules.

—**Mike T., Camden, New Jersey**

types of grants

Great, you've got a worthy project in need of funding. But before you go rushing off to bang out your proposal and look for donors, know this: There are many different types of grants, and one size does not fit all. Here is a list of basic grant types. Which one is the best match for your project?

Program grants The money is used for a specific program, such as establishing a girls' softball team. This type is most common for group projects, especially for non-profit organizations.

Continuing support grants While most program grants are made for one year only, some are renewed for another year.

Start-up grants Also known as program development grants, this money is given to provide initial support for a project but not fund it entirely. Start-up grants (sometimes called seed money) help bring in more grants by showing other prospective donors a base of support.

Research grants These funds pay to study an issue, such as a cure for a disease. The grant money is often funneled through an institution, such as a hospital or university, which provides the research facilities and pays the salaries of the professional and research staff.

Scholarship grants and fellowships These grants cover expenses for undergraduate, graduate, or postgraduate education. They can be awarded to individuals or to institutions that pass them on to individuals. Graduate and postgraduate grants may be classified as fellowships.

Challenge or matching grants These grants boost contributions by requiring that part of a project's cost come from other funding sources, such as fund-raising or other grants.

Endowments Established with individual monetary gifts, and sometimes grants, endowments are invested to provide a continuous flow of interest income to support the cause. Large endowments are the best way to maintain a nonprofit organization.

Consulting grants Donors may pay for hiring a consultant on a project.

Conference grants Grant funds may be made available to set up and run conferences or seminars, or to send project officers to such meetings.

ASK THE EXPERTS

Why is so little grant money available to cover operating costs, such as salaries or overhead expenses?

Most grantmakers prefer to help start a project or give it a boost partway through, but not to cover any ongoing expenses once it is up and running. That is because most funders feel that once a project is started, its running costs should come from other efforts, such as endowments or membership drives.

What's available to cover the costs for buildings and equipment?

Actually, some donors will cover building costs, but they are in a minority. Donations of equipment are sometimes more readily available, particularly if the equipment is used or refurbished. This is known as an **in-kind donation**—in other words, a donation of something other than money. (For more on this, see page 66.)

I met someone recently who writes grant proposals for a living. How can this one job function expand into an entire job?

When the stakes are high, a professional grantwriter can easily earn his or her salary. Big nonprofit organizations often keep several grant proposal writers on staff or on retainer to target the right donors for specific projects and tailor proposals to win funding.

grant timeline

It's tough to calculate how long it takes to apply for a grant. There are so many factors that affect a schedule. Here are some of the more important ones to consider.

- **Your time** You may not be able to work on your proposal full time.

- **The size of the budget** A simple project requiring a small amount of money, say $5,000, won't take nearly as much time to write about as a complex project needing $100,000.

- **Your technical ability** You may be new to proposal writing and may know nothing about how to assemble a suitable budget.

- **Group input** A number of your colleagues may have to read the proposal and make suggestions.

Here's Approximately How Long Each Task Might Take

TASK	TIME
■ Working out the details of your project with colleagues (If you need to find a nonprofit sponsor, add 4 more weeks.)	1 day–4 weeks
■ Asking for letters of support	2 days–2 weeks
■ Writing the grant proposal	1–4 weeks
■ Researching potential donors and calling them for further information	1–3 weeks
■ Gathering all the paperwork to include with the proposal	1 day–1 week
■ Review by your colleagues	1 day–2 weeks
■ Time allowance for mail delivery (Some organizations require you to mail your proposal; others let you send it by e-mail.)	1 day–2 weeks
TOTAL	**3–18 weeks**

Most grants are given to serve needs in various categories. Before you start your research, consider all the categories that might apply to your grant. Here's a sample of some basic categories to use as keywords (descriptive words to type into an Internet search engine) when you begin looking for donors.

Grant Categories

Addiction and crisis centers

Animal welfare

Arts and culture

Community development

Disabled

Education (elementary, secondary, and higher)

Elderly

Environment

Filmmaking, media, and communication

Health and hospitals

Historic preservation

International projects

Libraries and information services

Mental health

Minorities

Recreation

Religion

Research

Scholarships, student aid, and student loans

Social services

Women and girls

Youth

Examples of Causes That Grants Help

Education (elementary, secondary, and higher)

Lift children out of poverty with aid from the i2 Foundation (**www.i2foundation.org**), founded by employees of i2 Technologies "to make a world of difference."

Filmmaking, Media, and Communication

Get up to $5,000 to self-publish a comic book from the Xeric Foundation (**www.xericfoundation.com**), founded by Peter A. Laird, cocreator of the Teenage Mutant Ninja Turtles.

Health and Hospitals

Receive support for cancer research or to improve a young cancer patient's life from the Kristen Ann Carr Fund (**www.sarcoma.com**), named for a 22-year-old woman who died of sarcoma, a rare form of cancer.

Mental Health

Undergo psychoanalysis to develop your creativity with financial support from the Lucy Daniels Foundation (**www.ldf.org**), whose founder, a writer and psychologist, says, "Psychoanalysis saved my writing and my life."

Recreation

Start a children's soccer team in your neighborhood with money from the U.S. Soccer Foundation (**www.ussoccerfoundation.org**).

now what do I do?

Answers to common questions

I was looking through a list of grants and saw that the donors had a lot of restrictions about whom they will help. How can I work around some of those restrictions?

You can't. Nearly all foundations impose some restrictions on their grants to filter out causes they don't want to support. Many want to fund organizations only within the donor's home state. Others apply their grants only to a certain portion of the population, such as the elderly or Native Americans. Still others limit their giving to seed-money grants and don't offer any other kinds of funding. Knowing those restrictions and limitations is key to finding the right donor. If you don't fit the grant requirements like a glove, just move on to the next donor.

Are a grant proposal and a grant application the same?

Not exactly. The information is essentially the same in a proposal and an application, but the format is different. A grant application is a form with questions that the prospective donor sends to you to answer. Government agencies use grant applications. A grant proposal is a narrative that tells about the problem you seek to remedy, how you propose to do it, and with whom (see chapter 3). Follow the donor's guidelines.

How many pages is a proposal or an application likely to be?

An application for a government agency is likely to be 20 to 30 pages, including many extra attachments. Proposals for foundations run 6 to 10 pages long, and have just a few attachments. Proposals for corporate grants are usually the shortest—no more than six pages is often recommended, and shorter is preferable. Some funders will ask for a **letter of intent,** also known as a **letter of inquiry,** a three-to-five-page overview of the project (see more on page 146), before you submit the full proposal.

What makes a grant proposal stand out from the others?

Funders like to see that you are working with other nonprofits and have support from your community. Donors look to fund interesting and original projects. They also favor projects that solve a pressing problem, such as a sports program designed to curb a rise in a community's gang-related crime.

Now Where Do I Go?

CONTACTS

The Foundation Center
www.fdncenter.org

The Association of Fundraising Professionals
www.afpnet.org

The Nonprofit Resource Center
www.not-for-profit.org

BOOKS

America's Nonprofit Sector:
A Primer, 2nd Edition

A Nonprofit Organization Operating Manual:
Planning for Survival and Growth
By Arnold J. Olenick and Philip R. Olenick

Directory of Operating Grants, 6th Edition

Directory of Building and Equipment Grants,
6th Edition

Directory of Computer and Software Grants,
4th Edition

Directory of Grants for Organizations Serving
People with Disabilities, 11th Edition

Directory of Health Grants, 2nd Edition

The Foundation Center's Guide
to Proposal Writing, 3rd Edition
By Jane C. Geever

National Guide to Funding in Religion,
6th Edition

National Guide to Funding for Libraries and
Information Services, 6th Edition

National Guide to Funding in Higher
Education, 6th Edition

Foundation Giving Trends: Update on Funding
Priorities

National Guide to Funding in Arts and Culture,
7th Edition

National Guide to Funding in Health,
7th Edition

National Guide to Funding in Aging,
6th Edition

National Guide to Funding for the
Environment and Animal Welfare, 6th Edition

The PRI Directory: Charitable Loans and
Other Program-Related Investments by
Foundations

Foundation Grants to Individuals, 12th Edition
(also available on CD-ROM)

Grant Writing for Dummies
By Bev Browning

The Complete Guide to Getting a Grant: How
to Turn your Ideas into Dollars
By Laurie Blum

Secrets of Successful Grantsmanship: A
Guerrilla Guide to Raising Money
By Susan L. Golden

Finding a sponsor

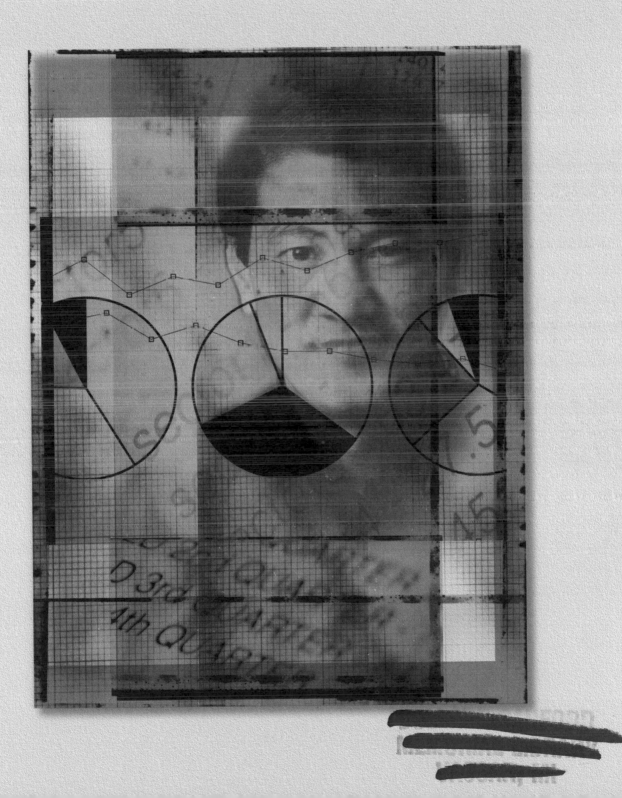

a nonprofit partner

The secret to getting the most for your cause

Most grantmaking foundations give only to nonprofit organizations that have filed for tax-exempt status with the IRS and have been designated a 501(c)3. So what if your project is not affiliated with a library or registered charity? (If you already have nonprofit status, you can skip this section!) Even if your cause is a good one, such as staging nighttime summer basketball games to keep kids off the streets, if you don't have a nonprofit sponsor, you will have a hard time getting grant money to fund it.

But take heart. You may already be only one step away from qualifying for grant money. If you have worked with a nonprofit organization in the past, even as a volunteer, you could ask them to take on your project as part of their ongoing services to the community. With a nonprofit ally, you can apply for grants for your projects.

Even if you don't think you're affiliated with a nonprofit, you may be. Do any of the following roles apply to you?

- Do you volunteer at your children's school?

- Are you a board member for your community library?

- Are you an employee of a YMCA or YWCA?

- Do you act as an usher for your religious group?

If so, these affiliations may give you a chance to apply for grant money.

ASK THE EXPERTS

My sponsor has just applied for nonprofit status, so it has no 501(c)3 letter from the IRS yet. Do I have to wait until it comes before sending out grant proposals?

No, unless the donor specifically says otherwise, you can send a copy of the group's application with your grant proposals. Once the IRS sends a letter granting 501(c)3 status, you can forward a copy of the letter to your potential donors.

I want to get a grant for a local public school project. I'm getting blank looks from the school administration when I ask for a copy of a 501(c)3 letter. How do I get a school's 501(c)3 letter?

You don't need a 501(c)3 letter to qualify for grants for public schools. The nonprofit status of a government-funded school is a given. The same applies to grants for other government-funded organizations, such as state-run universities and hospitals. Religious organizations may also be covered by this exception. But don't assume that all education establishments get the same treatment: You still need to show nonprofit documentation for fee-charging private schools.

finding the right partner

Like minds, similar causes

Your project needs a sponsoring nonprofit organization to qualify for grant funds. But where can you find a nonprofit that shares your goals? Simple—do a little research. Scout around your local nonprofit agencies and read their brochures or annual reports. (For more on that, see page 88.)

Most nonprofit organizations are very upfront about describing their aims, goals, and the people they want to help. The majority of nonprofits publish a formal **mission statement** (a paragraph or two that outlines why they exist, what they do, and whom they serve). Check for this statement at the nonprofit's Web site, or ask for the group's brochures or documents at your local library. If you have been working or volunteering for a nonprofit group, and you want them to sponsor your project, ask to see a copy of their mission statement.

With the mission statement in one hand and your project details in the other, do a little comparison. How does the nonprofit's mission statement compare with the objectives of your project? Do they fall within the parameters of the mission statement? That's a good sign, but there's another thing to check out: Is there any possible conflict between your project and anything your potential partner is doing?

If there isn't a good match, you have two choices: Look for a more compatible sponsor or make some adjustments to your project to reflect the group's mission.

Ways to Work With a Sponsor

If a nonprofit group agrees to sponsor your project, it will assume control of it in a very real way. But this does not mean you'll be left out of the picture. Here are some roles that let you stay involved.

Volunteer You agree to donate your time and expertise to the group on a pro bono basis. The nonprofit is still in charge, but you retain a role that you and the group agree on.

Consultant In this role, you are not directly employed by the nonprofit group that's managing your project, but you are paid a fee for handling certain aspects of the job. The nonprofit retains control, but you will have various responsibilities, depending on your consulting contract with the organization.

Employee As an employee of a nonprofit organization, it will be part of your job to work on your project. You may be a temporary employee whose role at the nonprofit lasts for the duration of the project. Or you may be a permanent staffer, assigned to certain duties on the project but called upon to work on other programs later. In this scenario, the project is under the authority of the group, but you have some degree of responsibility and control over it, ranging from being practically autonomous to being closely supervised by the nonprofit's staff.

Get Proof

When you interview potential sponsors for your project, make sure they are bona fide nonprofit organizations. Ask to see a copy of their most recent 501(c)3 letter from the IRS. Getting proof in writing early on will ensure that you are dealing with an organization that can help your project get funded.

paying for a partner

Get help and automatic nonprofit status

If you can't find a nonprofit sponsor to take you on, consider paying a fee to partner with a nonprofit group. Essentially, you are paying the sponsoring group for the privilege of using their nonprofit status, and they provide you with the service of funneling the funds you receive from foundations.

Two organizations that will act as fiscal agents for groups that do not have nonprofit status are the New York Foundation for the Arts at **www.nyfa.org** (212-366-6900, or e-mail nyfaweb@nyfa.org) and the Tides Center in San Francisco at **www.tidescenter.org** (415-561-6300, or e-mail info@tides.org).

The good news is that when you are connected with a well-established nonprofit organization, you are more likely to get more and larger grants. The bad news is that the nonprofit usually wants a percentage of any grant money you receive for your project. The size of the nonprofit's cut depends on how much the sponsoring group will do for you. If it acts only as a fiscal pass-

through for your funding, the fee is likely to be anywhere between 3% and 10% to cover their administrative costs. If the group offers you office space, equipment, or the help of administrative staff, your costs will go up proportionally. This type of arrangement is called a partial association, and it can be well worth your while.

When you find an organization that agrees to sponsor your project, it's time to draw up a **letter of agreement** covering the various aspects of your relationship. Because the stakes are high, don't sign any agreement until it's been read over and approved by a lawyer who specializes in nonprofit law.

Ask the Advice of a Lawyer

No matter how close your connection with a sponsor might be, always have a lawyer look over any letter of agreement you draw up with a nonprofit group before you sign it.

If you can't afford to retain your own lawyer, borrow one. Many law firms offer an attorney's time, for a small fee (or even free), to review contracts and other agreements for nonprofit organizations. Any lawyer in your community can probably tell you about a lawyers association whose members offer legal advice for free or for a nominal fee.

Here are some sources you can contact to find free or low-priced legal help for nonprofits.

www.corporateprobono.org
This Web site matches nonprofit organizations with lawyers across the country. It's run by the Pro Bono Institute at Georgetown University Law Center and the American Corporate Counsel Association.

www.vlany.org
Volunteer Lawyers for the Arts helps groups and individuals working in the arts. Although it's based in New York, it serves clients nationwide.

www.lany.org
The Lawyers Alliance for New York, as its name suggests, covers the New York area. It works to improve the quality of life in low-income and disadvantaged neighborhoods.

lawyers.martindale.com
Run by Martindale-Hubbell, this Web site lists most U.S. lawyers. Look in the "Lawyer Locator" section for a tab labeled "Location/Area of Practice" and enter your city or county and state. Then, in the window designated "enter specific area of practice," type one of these terms: charitable giving, charitable organizations law, charitable trusts and foundations, nonprofit organizations law, nonprofit tax law, private foundations, public charities, and tax-exempt organizations.

starting a nonprofit

Form a tax-exempt organization for your cause

You're one of the lucky ones. Your project is growing by leaps and bounds. Even without a nonprofit sponsor, you have raised thousands of dollars to keep it going. Good for you! But this level of success breeds its own problems: Now you need office space, a dedicated phone line, and administrative help. And worse, you will have to pay taxes on any of the money you've raised that you can't expense or don't spend.

Maybe it's time to consider converting your project into a nonprofit organization. When you form your own nonprofit, it gives you tax-exempt nonprofit status, which can greatly expand your funding options. If your project has an operating budget of more than $25,000 and you plan to keep it running for a number of years, nonprofit status will be a boon. Just be aware that the process takes about three months and requires lots of continuing documentation.

If you decide to organize your own nonprofit agency, first get the advice of a lawyer, preferably one with nonprofit experience (see page 31) to help you with these steps.

Incorporate You will need to incorporate your group as a nonprofit entity. This means writing up your purpose or mission as well as appointing a board of directors and setting a schedule for them to meet regularly. It also means creating a budget and appointing a treasurer to report your finances to the IRS. Regulations differ from state to state, so be sure you use a local lawyer for this step.

Apply for nonprofit tax-exempt status You will need to apply for 501(c)3 status from the IRS. This will meet the requirement of most donors, many of whom only give to 501(c)3 groups because it is one way they can receive a tax deduction. It also provides a measure of your group's authenticity.

Plan for Graceful Endings

As you write the documents you need to form your own nonprofit group, such as articles of incorporation and bylaws, be sure to plan for what happens if the group disbands. Even if such a possibility seems remote, the regulations should contain information about how the nonprofit will be ended and who will take responsibility for filing the last financial statements.

A SK THE EXPERTS

I want to market a creative toy I've invented. Can I establish a nonprofit organization to manufacture and sell it?

Ask yourself this: Are you just trying to avoid paying taxes, or is there a charitable purpose associated with your toy? Associate a marketable product with a nonprofit organization only if you want all monetary benefits—and all your efforts—to be put to charitable uses. If you later transfer any assets and patents developed by the nonprofit group to any individual or to a profit-making organization, then the income will be taxed as unrelated business income. If there is no charitable aspect to your toy, it's better to create a traditional for-profit business.

How much does it cost to become a nonprofit organization?

The expenses fall into two categories: state filing fees and legal fees. Nonprofits should incorporate in the same state as their headquarters. Filing fees differ by state. Many states charge less than $100 to incorporate a nonprofit organization, but some, including Arkansas and Pennsylvania, top $200. Legal fees also vary, but for a straightforward filing, expect to pay about $100-$200.

FIRST PERSON DISASTER STORY
We're Pooped

It was just going to be a little nonprofit organization. My husband and I, both newly retired, thought it would be a smart way to fund our genealogical searches for our families. We didn't ask any legal advice, just went ahead and did it. We managed to get through the incorporation procedure and obtain our nonprofit status as an educational group devoted to the history of the area. We even got a few grants from some local businesses, and, of course, our own families donated money. But what we didn't realize was that being a nonprofit required board meetings and financial reports, not to mention fund-raising efforts. Our operation really wasn't big enough to warrant becoming a nonprofit. I wish we had spoken with a nonprofit lawyer so we would have understood the work involved.

—Lily F., Fort Worth, Texas

now what do I do?

Answers to common questions

When I was interviewing a possible sponsoring organization for a reading series, they offered me a job on their staff to run practically the same project I was planning. Is this a good idea?

It can be, if the organization is sound and has a good reputation, and if you like the job as they describe it. After all, they will then take over the fund-raising and the administration and leave you to devote yourself to the job you hoped to accomplish in the first place—with fringe benefits. But get it all in writing as a job description in your contract. That way, if their personnel and priorities change, you won't suddenly find yourself switched to another project without your consent.

I have been asked to be a member of the board of directors for a nonprofit organization. What will that require?

You will meet with the other board members periodically to review the activities of the group. Be prepared to be involved in fund-raising. You will have fiscal as well as moral responsibility to make sure the group operates within its bylaws and fulfills its mission. You'll serve on committees; review financial reports, budgets, and audits; and oversee the management of investments. You and your contacts will help bring in volunteers and attract more donors. Be sure to ask about insurance covering the board to protect you from any liability as a result of the nonprofit's actions.

I'm in the process of incorporating a nonprofit historical society to preserve an old family home as a museum. Can I ask several family members to serve as board members?

You can ask whomever you want to serve on the board, but have at least as many outsiders as family members. Potential donors prefer to see a variety of backgrounds among board members. To get a good mix, consider professional specialists in your field (to act as advisers on projects), prominent businesspeople (for fiscal oversight), community members (representative of those who will benefit from your services), and well-known fund-raisers in the community (to help bring in more financial support).

I started my nonprofit reading program in Maryland, but I want to conduct the project in Washington, D.C. Will that be a problem?

Laws of incorporation vary from state to state, and even within states there may be several types of nonprofit corporations. Check with your state's charity registration office and your legal adviser.

Now Where Do I Go?

CONTACTS

The Internet Nonprofit Center's
FAQ for start-ups
www.nonprofits.org/npofaq/

Starting a Nonprofit Organization:
One-Stop Answer Page
nonprofit.about.com/library/weekly/
blonestart.htm

The Alliance for Nonprofit Management
www.allianceonline.org

Board Source FAQ "How do we become a
nonprofit organization?" www.boardsource.org

Tax Information for Charitable Organizations
The Internal Revenue Service

BOOKS

Tax Planning and Compliance for Tax-Exempt
Organizations: Forms, Checklists, Procedures
By Jody Blazek

Starting and Managing a Nonprofit
Organization: A Legal Guide, 3rd Edition
By Bruce R. Hopkins

The Nonprofit Board's Guide to Bylaws:
Creating a Framework for Effective
Governance
By Kim Arthur Zeitlin and Susan E. Dorn

The Nonprofit Handbook: Management,
3rd Edition
Edited by Tracy Daniel Conners

Starting and Running a Nonprofit
Organization
By Joan M. Hummel

How to Form a Nonprofit Corporation
in All 50 States, 4th Edition
By Anthony Mancuso

The Complete Guide to Nonprofit Corporations
By Ted Nicholas

A Nonprofit Organization Operating Manual:
Planning for Survival and Growth
By Arnold J. Olenick and Philip R. Olenick

Fundraising Fundamentals: A Guide to Annual
Giving for Professionals and Volunteers
By James M. Greenfield

Writing a proposal

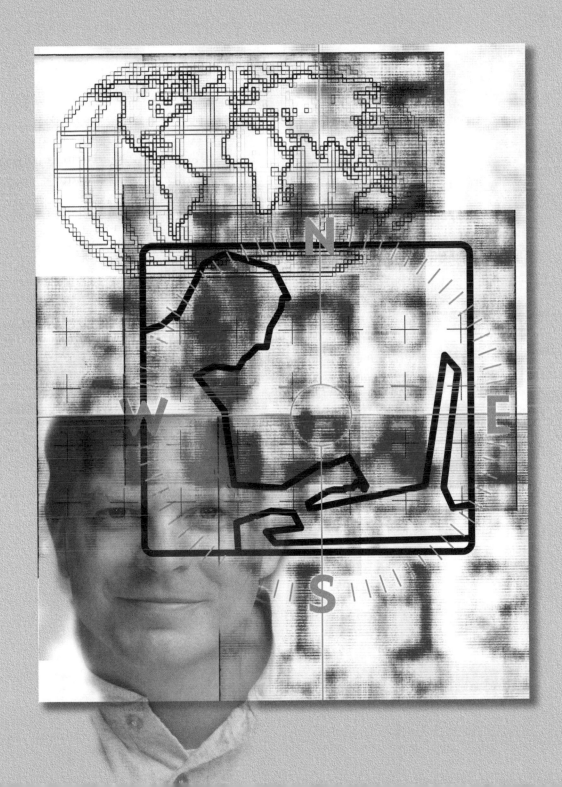

the boilerplate proposal

The top 10 things your grant proposal needs

Right now, you know it all. You know your project cold. You know what you need to get it done. Your task: Tell donors all about it. And your first step is to write a **boilerplate**, or standardized, grant proposal. Once you have that in place, you'll have something to show the donors you'll find (more about that in chapter 5). If you are good at multitasking, you can write your proposal and search for donors at the same time—but don't skimp on either task. They're both crucial.

If you've never seen a grant proposal before, you'll probably be surprised at how straightforward it is. Grant proposals consist of 10 basic sections, including supporting materials.

TIP: When you're writing your own boilerplate, approach the sections in the order listed here, with one exception: Save the Introduction for last. You'll have a clearer idea of what to say once you've worked through the other sections.

- Introduction
  - Statement of Need
    - Goal
      - Objectives
        - Program Activities
          - Evaluation
            - History of the Organization and Its Funding
              - Summary or Conclusion
                - Project Budget
                  - Supporting Material
                    (resumé and press clippings)

ASK THE EXPERTS

I have never written a grant proposal before, and I am worried that I won't be any good at it. What do I do?

Grantwriting isn't all that hard, but it does mean entering into a new world with different rules and vocabulary. If you want a little help, consider taking a class on grantwriting; your local college may offer such courses, and the Foundation Center conducts them all over the country. Check out their Web site (**www.fdncenter.org**) to learn more about when and where they hold grantwriting classes. Hospitals, colleges, and universities often have grantwriters on staff who might mentor you. Also, the Association of Fundraising Professionals (**www.afpnet.org**) may have a chapter near you. Ask for mentoring help.

The nonprofit organization I volunteer for needs a grant, and no one has the time to write a proposal. Can we hire a freelance grantwriter?

Sure. Many experienced grantwriters work on a freelance basis. You can find a list of them on the Foundation Center's Web site. You can also check with the American Association of Fundraising Counsel at 800-462-2372 or **www.aafrc.org** for information regarding freelance writers. Grantwriters usually charge by the proposal. A few charge a fee based on a percentage of the grant money obtained, but members of the Association of Fundraising Professionals oppose percentage-based rates because of ethical reasons. Be sure to find out the writer's track record before hiring; make sure the writer's experience matches the size and scope of your project.

Do I write a different proposal for each foundation I want to apply to?

Yes, but it's not as hard as it sounds. Once you have a basic boilerplate proposal in place, you edit it to address the needs and concerns of each prospective donor foundation (see page 142). See more proposal samples beginning on page 184.

The Name Game

When choosing a name for your project, remember: Simple is best. It's fun to be cute and clever, but it's more important to be clear. Your project's name is the first contact people will have with your program. Keep it clear and informative. That way, it's more likely to attract interest.

Small Wonders
(Cute but obscure)

**Helping Hand
Child Care**
(Clear and useful)

describing the need

What wrongs do you intend to right?

The first step is to explain why the world needs your project. And when you make your **statement of need** (your description of the importance of your project), one rule reigns supreme: Be as specific as possible. Narrow down your statement of need as far as you can—the exact neighborhood, the precise age group, and other concrete descriptions. After reading this, a stranger should know exactly what problem you hope to set right, who will benefit, and where they are based. See examples of grant-winning proposals beginning on page 184.

But don't cram everything into this statement. You don't have to describe your project here. That comes later.

One trick that works well is to use statistics to support your statement of need. If children are lagging behind in school, cite area reading scores and compare them geographically. Look for any corroborating data such as demographic information, census numbers, and statistics. Any government studies in the area are especially helpful.

Another good way to underscore the need you describe is to quote a recognized source. Has a well-respected person spoken out against the problem? If so, add a short quote to your statement of need. Attachments are also helpful. Does a recent newspaper or magazine article describe the need you hope to address? Enclose a copy of any relevant clips with your proposal, and let them do some of the work for you.

TIP: Highlight the people you'll help, not your organization. It's not that your organization needs a new handicapped-access van. The need is that seven children who are developmentally disabled cannot go to the community park or school because they have no safe, reliable transportation.

Writing Tips: Statement of Need

When you're looking for information to support your statement of need, be sure to do your research thoroughly. Use the following criteria for choosing sources.

■ **Be timely** Out-of-date information will undermine your credibility. Do your homework to make sure you have the very latest available statistics.

■ **Be specific** If your program is in the Chicago area, focus your information hunt on Chicago. If you can, break it down by neighborhood. The more focused, the better.

■ **Be brief** You'll make your case best by focusing on only one or two strong points.

Sample

Check out this sample statement of need. It establishes the need succinctly and with just enough detail to be compelling.

According to the governor's Annual Report on Primary Education, 57% of the children in Thursdon Hills cannot read at grade level at the end of their first school year. Yet the reading levels can be improved with tutoring support, which is not currently available to Thursdon Hills first graders. Marlin Cary, director of the primary program at the state education department, says that reading scores can be improved by 30% to 60% if extra tutoring is given to children during the first grade.

what's your goal ?

Let them know what you want to achieve

The next two steps in your proposal are similar, but not the same. A proposal's goal and its objectives belong together, and it helps to write them at the same time, but they are different in important ways.

The **goal** is a general statement. It's the outcome you hope for. It's a vision thing, and that means it's short on detail. In fact, it's the shortest section in the whole proposal, because it must be clear enough to be expressed in a single sentence.

A good example of a goal is "to eliminate teen drug use in your neighborhood." It's hard to argue against it, and also hard to see how you plan to do it. But the details belong in the next section, the objectives.

The **objectives** are a series of specific statements that fill in the details that the goal doesn't have. Most proposals include two or three concrete objectives for a program. They list the specific ways you plan to reach your goal.

The main difference between your goal and your objectives is that goals cannot be measured and objectives can. In fact, your objectives can be measured so specifically that you will cite the dates and numbers you're aiming for.

It's easy to see how your goals and objectives are related, but they must work together to support the statement of need that opens your proposal. Make sure your objectives support your goals. Then make sure that both answer the need statement. If they do, congratulations. You're getting closer to winning your grant.

TIP: Use numbers or bullets to make your proposal easier to read.

Writing Tips: Goal and Objectives

■ Your goal is your final destination; your objectives are what you use to get there.

■ The objectives specify how you intend to reach your goal.

Here and below are examples from a proposal for the hypothetical Growing Great Readers Project showing how these elements relate to each other.

Sample

This goal is a good general statement: It addresses a need that exists and is hard to argue against, but it does not say specifically how the need will be met.

The goal of the Growing Great Readers Project is to help first-grade children in Thursdon Hills become better readers.

Sample

Each objective is measurable: The comparative reading scores, the number of students, and the number of parents.

The objectives of the Growing Great Readers Project are:

■ To offer a new after-school tutoring program aimed at improving reading scores for first graders at Thursdon Hills Elementary School.

■ To enroll at least 50% of the first-grade children in the tutoring program (the first graders number approximately 50 each fall).

■ To arrange for at least one parent of each child to attend a tutoring workshop to help support the child's reading efforts at home.

accomplishing your objectives

The heart of your proposal— the program activities

How do you plan to meet the objectives you've just outlined? Ah, there's the crucial question. And it's the program activities section in your proposal that needs to answer it.

Here, you describe exactly what you plan to do. Explain how you will reach each of your objectives—and, most important of all, keep your writing to the point. Describe your time frame, the activities you propose, and the staff (or volunteers) you'll require. Use a few relevant details, such as training your staff might need, any special supplies or equipment, and publicity. You needn't go into great detail here, but do mention items crucial for the success of the project.

A good way to help you organize your thoughts is to go through each of your objectives in order. Ask yourself, "What must be done in order to accomplish this objective?" List one to three activities needed to make it happen.

Writing Tips: Program Activities

In this section, describe the activities that will accomplish your project's objectives.

- Be specific.
- Include dates, schedules, and the titles of people involved in the work.

Sample

Note that the major activities are briefly listed and that they fulfill the three objectives for the project (see page 43). The donor wants to know the basics of how the project will run, but without a lot of details.

At the beginning of August, a director with an MS in primary reading development will start the Growing Great Readers Project. She will talk with first-grade teachers at Thursdon Hills Elementary School in order to coordinate the project's tutoring program with the school's lesson plans. The director will train 30 volunteers from the Richardson Retirement Community.

Media releases and TV appearances by the director will advertise the Growing Great Readers Project in August, and explain how the project can benefit all children. When parents come to register their first graders at the end of August, leaflets describing the tutoring sessions and the parent workshops will direct them to an enrollment desk. The director and volunteers will contact parents who do not enroll, explaining how the project can benefit each child.

During the school term, the first graders will meet with a trained volunteer twice a week after school to work on reading skills in the school cafeteria.

Three nights a week, the director will conduct repeat workshops to help parents hone their children's reading skills at home.

evaluating your project

How did you do?

Donors need to know that their money is being well spent. How will they know that? By having your project evaluated. Your proposal must include the way you will objectively measure how close you come to accomplishing the objectives you've stated. Sometimes that assessment is simple—an attendance tally, a collection of news clippings, or a report of lab results. Other times it may require summaries of reviews, user comments, or other, more complicated evaluations. And don't forget: If you need to pay for tests to measure your project's progress, make sure that expense is included in your budget. Meanwhile, most donors require periodic updates on projects, so prepare for a lot of letter writing.

FIRST PERSON DISASTER STORY
Getting Help

When the school term ended, I suddenly realized I hadn't yet gotten around to sending in the quarterly results on our tutoring program for first-grade readers. I had just been so busy keeping everyone's schedule on target that I had forgotten all about it. I quickly pulled together the stats and sent a final report to our donor with a note apologizing for missing the midterm reports. To make things worse, the results for the year were merely okay, because seven students bused in from another district couldn't stay after school for tutoring. Then the donor program director told me he could have funded transportation for those kids had I only handed in my reports on time. I was dumbstruck. I'll never let a progress report slide again.

—Annette S., Houston, Texas

Writing Tips: Evaluation

This section explains how the effects of the Growing Great Readers Project will be measured and how the results will be communicated to the donor.

Sample

Each of the three objectives (page 43) is assigned a measurement.

State when reports will be filed (in red)

Tell how and when objectives will be measured

During the first week of school, we will send a report on the number of students enrolled in the Growing Great Readers Project to the XYZ Foundation, as well as the number of parents who have signed up for the parent workshops. Attendance records for the tutoring sessions and the parent workshops will be forwarded at three-month intervals.

During the year, arrangements can be made for staff members from the XYZ Foundation to observe sessions in progress.

At the end of the school term, when the first-grade reading scores are released throughout the state, a complete report on the project will be submitted to the XYZ Foundation. The report will compare the Thursdon Hills Elementary School first-grade scores for the current year with those from the previous year.

Comparative ranking with other schools in the state will be analyzed. Summaries of reactions from both parents and teachers will also be included in the final report.

selling your organization

**What makes
you stand out?**

You're almost there. You've written out your goals and objectives and showed how they'll be measured. Now's the time to tell why your organization is the right group to run the show. Start by stating the mission of your organization—something you will find in the declaration that every nonprofit makes to the IRS.

Next, give a brief history of your organization. Start with the year it was founded and write one or two sentences about how your group has developed since then. Then, explain how the group operates, what its programs and projects are, and how it's funded. Keep it short and to the point, but make it clear that your program is the smart choice.

Find as much evidence as you can of wide support for your organization. Attach press articles about your group. And don't be afraid to ask for help: Get letters of support from your local political leaders, expressing confidence in your organization and describing the benefits your new project gives to the community.

TIP: If you have a great article about your organization but it includes some errors, put an asterisk by each mistake and type the correct information on the copy. You'll will get the benefit of good press, stop the spread of inaccurate information, and show the importance your organization places on truth.

Writing Tips: History of Your Organization

Prove your organization is capable of making your project an unqualified success.

Sample

Give founding date

Founded in 1988, the Thursdon Hills Elementary School Parent Teacher Association is dedicated to improving the learning experience of every child in the school. It coordinates the efforts of parents with those of their teachers.

State the organization's mission

Since its inception, the Thursdon Hills PTA has raised funds for projects such as parent workshops on how to help with homework; teacher-upgrade seminars in reading, science, math, and art; and field trips for the students to museums and performing arts events. Its ongoing used-computer purchase plan has expanded the computer room equipment from the 20 stations provided by the state to 30 stations. In-kind donations of six television sets and VCR's solicited from local merchants have allowed teachers to add video programs to their lesson plans.

Indicate community support

The present reading-assistance program consists of parents privately paying teacher aides for assisting their children during after-school hours.

List fundraising sources

The Thursdon Hills Elementary School PTA receives its operating expenses from state funds allotted by the legislature. Most of its other funding comes from parent membership donations (60% of the parents are members of the PTA, and of those, 80% are donors). Other funds come from special events such as bake sales, used-clothing sales, and garage sales.

Note that the percentage of membership donations is particularly impressive.

summing it up

Opening and closing

You're on the home stretch. There's only one more step to go. Actually, that's two more steps, but it's basically the same information written twice—once for the **introduction** and once for the **summary** or **conclusion** that appears at the end of the proposal.

Why did you have to save the intro for last? Well, you have to get through the other sections to have the best perspective on your project. Once you've written down all the details, you'll be able to write a more concise statement about the project as a whole. And the summary basically repeats the message of the introduction.

For better or worse, the introduction and summary are the most important parts of your proposal. Each section plays an important part, but the introduction and the summary are crucial. Program officers at donor foundations are very busy, and they may not read all of every proposal that crosses their desks. They often decide whether to proceed based on the introduction or summary. Make them clear and precise so your proposal passes to the next step. See examples of two more grant proposals beginning on page 184.

Writing Tips: Introduction

In a paragraph, state who you are, what the problem is, how you propose to fix it—and your organization's qualifications for the job. Begin by reading over the sections you have already written. Mention the amount of money you want, and be sure to work in the name of the donor you are applying to. Make it straightforward. Try to use action verbs to make it sound lively. For instance:

Sample

> The reading test scores of children in Graham County are nearly the lowest in the state. To improve performance, the Parent Teacher Association of Thursdon Hills Elementary School is establishing an educational project called Growing Great Readers. With support from the XYZ Foundation in the amount of $45,000, we will create a tutorial program in which volunteers from the local retirement home will help to improve the reading scores of our first graders.

Writing Tips: Summary

In closing, sum up what you have said in the proposal. It will be similar to the introduction, but express it in different words. Add a warm, somewhat emotional appeal. Try to give the prospective donor a reason for helping you with your project.

Sample

> With the generous help of the XYZ Foundation in the amount of $45,000, we will address the substandard reading performance of the children of the Thursdon Hills Elementary School with our Growing Great Readers Project. We will train volunteer tutors to coach our first graders in a way that will enhance the teachers' efforts. We will advise our parents on how to enrich their children's reading experiences at home. These projects will allow our students to establish a sound foundation in reading skills and enable them to perform more consistently in every subject throughout their school years.

supporting material

Show how much support you already have

Writing a grant is a bit like applying for a job—you want to put your best foot forward. How do you do that? Well, just as you would do for a job, get letters of recommendation. And be sure to ask for them early—it can take time for people to write them.

Start with your local political leaders. Ask your mayor or the president of your town council to write a letter endorsing your project and your nonprofit organization. You want them to help you make a case for your project. If you can, get letters of endorsement from your congressperson and senator.

Once you have a letter of support from a civic leader, ask for letters of endorsement from those who would be affected by your project. For example, if your project is to fund a middle school reading program, ask for letters of support from the board of education and the superintendent of schools. A few earnest letters from middle school teachers might be important, too.

Hopefully, your nonprofit organization has garnered a few press clippings about its work. Collect those in a file, then see which ones are relevant to your proposal. Make copies of these to include with it. Also, consider press stories that underscore the need for your project. For instance, an article alerting readers to the increasing rate of teenage drug use in your town would be ideal to include with a proposal for a project designed to help teens stay off drugs.

Next, consider the people who will be working on the project once it gets funded. If any have impressive academic or professional credentials, get copies of their resumés. You will want to send them out with your proposal.

The final piece of paper you will need to get is a copy of your nonprofit or nonprofit sponsor's 501(c)3 IRS tax-exempt letter.

ASK THE EXPERTS

How many letters of recommendation should I get?

You really need only two, possibly three. You don't want to flood your proposal with a slew of letters. The point you want to make is that you have community backing for your project.

I am still waiting for a letter of endorsement from my congresswoman. How long does it take to write one of these letters?

It doesn't take long to write them, but it may take a while to get the ball rolling. You can help things along in your request with a few tricks: Include key points about your project so that she can write about them. And give a deadline for when you need a reply. If it's clear you are not going to get a letter from one civic leader, move on to another. For this reason, it's always good to ask several people for letters. It's better to get more than you need and pick out the best ones for submission.

Can I offer to write the letter of recommendation and have the person sign it?

Yes, you can. To speed the process along, it is helpful to write a generic sample letter of endorsement about your project and mail, fax, or e-mail it to prospective endorsers. Tactfully, tell them they are welcome to use your exact words or pick and choose phrases and paragraphs as they see fit. Remind them to use their own letterhead and provide an original signature.

TIP: A letter from someone who has used your service often has the highest impact. If a parent or child sends you a note, ask for written permission to use it, then copy it. Don't retype or edit it. Use their thankful voice without interpretation. Let those who you've helped tell your story.

the budget summary

Is there a financial officer in the house?

Budgets are important. Really important. Foundations want to see that you have done your homework and know exactly the amount of money your project will need. And they will reject grants with unrealistic budgets immediately. So you may want to leave this part to a financial professional in the organization— the tax lawyer or accountant. If there is no such warm body, then you'll have to do it. First, set up some meetings with the key people involved and and get their financial input. You'll also need to include budgetary information on your nonprofit sponsor. (Because budgets are so important, read chapter 4 for a full discussion.) Meanwhile, here's what's likely to be included in most project budget summaries.

A list of your expenses

■ **Salaries and wages** If your proposal calls for hiring someone, indicate whether the position is full- or part-time, and don't forget benefits and payroll tax. Also list any expenses needed for training.

■ **Travel, equipment, printing, and copying** Try to estimate these costs as accurately as you can.

■ **Rent and utilities** These amounts are usually fixed.

A list of your revenue

■ **Other grants** List any that you have already secured from other funders.

■ **Individual donations**

■ **Fund-raising events and products**

■ **In-kind support** These are donated goods and services that will help support your project. Find the estimated value of volunteer time at **www.independentsector.org**. ($16.05 an hour in 2001)

Tip: The difference between your expenses and revenue is the amount you are seeking to be covered by grants. Do not ask one donor to fund your entire project. Instead ask several donors to fund various parts of your budget, for example, staffing or utilities.

To give you an idea about the possible items to list in your expenses and revenue columns, use this budget summary from the common grant application of the National Network of Grantmakers. Find it at www.nng.org. (For more information on the common grant application, see page 58.)

IV. BUDGET

If you already prepare organizational and project budgets that approximate this format, please feel free to submit them in their original forms. You may reproduce this form on your computer and/or submit separate pages for income and expenses.

Budget for the period: _____ to _____

EXPENSES			INCOME	
Item	Amount	FT/PT	Source	Amount
Salaries & wages (breakdown by individual	$_____	_____	Government grants & contracts (specify)	$
position and indicate full or part-time)	_____	_____	Foundations (specify)	$_____
	_____	_____	Corporations	$_____
	_____	_____	Religious Institutions	$_____
	_____	_____	United Way, Combined	$_____
Fringe benefits & payroll Taxes	$_____		Federal Campaign & other federated campaigns	
Consultants & professional fees	$_____			
Travel	$_____		Individual contributions	$_____
Equipment	$_____		Fundraising events	$_____
Supplies	$_____		& products	
Training	$_____		Membership income	$_____
Printing & copying	$_____		In-kind support	$_____
Telephone & fax	$_____		Other (earned income, consulting fees, etc. Please specify)	$_____
Postage & delivery	$_____			
Rent & utilities	$_____		_____	_____
In-kind expense	$_____		_____	_____
Other (specify)	$_____		_____	_____
_____				
TOTAL EXPENSE	$_____		TOTAL INCOME	$_____
			BALANCE	$_____

editing your proposal

Clarify and compress

Editing is one of the best-kept secrets of writing well. Good editing requires time and a little bit of patience. It's a good idea to let your proposal alone for a few days and then, and only then, read it over. You'll be surprised how objective you can be about your own writing after a little time has passed. Fix any redundant phrases you find. Clarify sentences.

Here are a few tips that may help.

■ **Read the proposal out loud to yourself** You can find a surprising number of "clunky" phrases this way. A sentence might look okay on the page, but when you try to say it, it turns out to be awkward or lacking in clarity.

■ **Look for ways to use action verbs instead of passive verbs** Instead of saying "afternoon classes will be taught by volunteers," try "volunteers will teach the afternoon classes." Add more life to your proposal.

■ **Don't be uncertain** Give your proposal a more decisive tone by removing "can," "might," and "hope to." "We can complete 50 samples each week" is not as strong as "We will complete 50 samples each week."

■ **Trim the proposal** You want to keep your writing straightforward and to the point. Eliminate any unnecessary phrases or lengthy descriptions.

■ **Check for readability** Find a friend who knows nothing about your grant needs or nonprofit sponsor. Ask your friend to review your grant to see if it is clear and understandable.

■ **Check for spelling errors, typos, and extra spaces** If you can, find someone who can proofread your proposal.

 # ASK THE EXPERTS

My own writing always sounds awful to me. Where can I go for help?

You may be overly self-critical—or you may be right. So ask someone to read your proposal for you, such as a friend who can write well. Or put a note on the bulletin board of a local college asking for an English major to edit your proposal for an hourly fee. Best of all, network to find and talk to others who have written proposals that helped them get grants.

I have a lot of interesting information about my project that I want to send to a possible donor. Why must the proposal be so short?

Pretend you're sitting at your desk behind a stack of proposals. There are 50 of them. Your job is to skim through them looking for stand-out projects. Time is tight. Now's not the time for bells and whistles. State your idea for your project clearly and quickly. If the idea interests the project officers, they will ask for more information. Then you can really go to town and provide as much information as you want.

TIP: Consider asking a former major donor to read your newest proposal. They will be flattered and will learn about your latest needs. Then let them know if you receive the grant. They might even want to contribute to your project.

a grant template

Step-by-step through a grant proposal

If it all seems overwhelming and you can't organize your thoughts, don't panic. Help is at hand from several excellent templates that you can use to help organize your writing. They are known as **common grant applications,** and you can download them onto your computer.

One of the more useful ones was created by the National Network of Grantmakers, a group of over 50 donors who share common philanthropic interests. Their application includes fill-in-the-blank forms for a cover sheet and budget, a narrative outline, and an attachments checklist. This can help you write a more cohesive proposal, and it's a standard form for applying to any of the donors in the network. (Think of it as a common application form for all the colleges on the East Coast—that's how valuable it is to grantseekers.) Check out their common grant application online at **www.nng.org**, and choose "common grant application."

You can check an index of other common grant applications at **www.fdncenter.org.** Click on Finding Funders, then click on Common Grant Applications (this will take you to the long Web address **fdncenter.org/funders/cga/index.html**). Use the list to obtain common forms, to find out if a donor you are targeting uses a common format, and to find other like-minded donors who accept the same format.

On the opposite page is a sample checklist for attachments from the common grant application created by the National Network of Grantmakers.

III. ATTACHMENTS/REQUIREMENTS (Supply everything checked below by funder who prepared this copy.)

A. Evaluation

☐ 1. Briefly describe your plan for evaluating the success of the project or for your organization's work. What questions will be addressed? Who will be involved in evaluating this work—staff, board, constituents, community, consultants? How will the evaluation results be used?

B. Organizational Structure/Administration

☐ 1. Briefly describe how your organization works: What are the responsibilities of board, staff and volunteers?
And if membership organization, define criteria for membership. Are there dues?

☐ 2. Who will be involved in carrying out the plans outlined in this request? Include a brief paragraph summarizing the qualifications of key individuals involved.

☐ 3. Provide a list of your board of directors with related demographic information.

☐ 4. How is the board selected, who selects them and how often?

☐ 5. Include an organizational chart showing decision-making structure.

C. Finances

☐ 1. Most recent, completed full year organizational financial statement (expenses, revenue and balance sheet), audited, if available.

☐ 2. Organization's current annual operating budget (See attached budget format).

☐ 3. Current project budget, other than general support (See attached format).

☐ 4. Projected operating budget for upcoming year (See attached format).

☐ 5. List individually other funding sources for this request. Include amounts and whether received, committed or projected/pending.

☐ 6. Describe your plans for future fund raising.

☐ 7. A copy of your IRS 501(c)(3) letter. If you do not have 510(c)(3) status, check with the funder to see if they are willing to fund through your fiscal sponsor or are willing to exercise expenditure responsibility. Additional information may be required to do so.

☐ 8. Other

D. Other Supporting Material

☐ 1. Letters of support/commitment (up to three).

☐ 2. Recent newsletter articles, newspaper clippings, evaluations or reviews (up to three).

☐ 3. Recent annual report.

☐ 4. Videos/cassettes are accepted ONLY if this box is checked.

☐ 5. Other

Guidelines for applicants (completed by funder)

Send ___ number of complete copies: cover sheet, five page proposal and attachments that are checked off.

Use a standard typeface no smaller than 10 points and no less than .25 in margins .

Proposals by fax are ☐ are not ☐ accepted.

Binders or folders are ☐ are not ☐ accepted.

Your proposal must be ☐ double sided ☐ single sided ☐ no preference.

Please use the following paper ☐ white/very light colored, ☐ recycled,
☐ 8½ x11 inches only, ☐ no preference.

Sí, aceptamos las solicitudes de fondos en español . ☐ Yes, we accept funding proposals in Spanish.

No aceptamos las solicitudes en español. ☐ No, we do not accept funding proposals in Spanish.

Funder who prepared this copy of the Common Grant Application: _____

now what do I do?

Answers to common questions

Several foundations have sent me application forms to fill out in lieu of writing proposals. Should I skip writing out a boilerplate proposal?

You can, but that's not something an expert would advise you to do. The process of writing a proposal will help you think through your project from a funder's point of view. And there's another benefit: You can also use sections from your basic proposal to fill in the application forms that some foundations require. Chances are, if your application is accepted, the funder will want to see more information, in which case you will send off your tailored boilerplate proposal. For examples of grant-winning proposals, see pages 184-193.

I don't type well. Can I write my proposal neatly by hand?

Draft your proposal however you work best, but be prepared to have it typed by someone. You cannot submit handwritten proposals.

I still don't see how to tell the goal from the objectives. Aren't they all the same thing in different words?

No, each is different. The goal is the overall aim of your project (a lunch program for summer campers). The objectives tell the specific measures to be used to achieve that aim (recruiting five volunteers to make lunch one day a week for four weeks).

Can I pump up the numbers a bit to help my organization at the end of the year?

It's not a good idea. Unless it's part of the arrangement you have with your donor, you won't be allowed to throw "leftover" funds into your general budget. Every cent you get must be used as outlined in the project grant. If you overestimate, you'll only have to give it back—which will make the donor think twice about your next proposal. Get as close to actual costs as possible in your budget request. If you have a small amount left over, ask the donor if you should return it. Some donors will allow you to spend it on added "special items" related to the project. Some will let you apply it toward the project's next annual budget.

What if our project runs into unexpected expenses?

If legitimate unforeseen expenses crop up, go back to the donor and tell them the situation. If they seem sensitive to the turn of events, then ask for more money. If they don't have the funds, they may be able to steer you toward someone who does. Foundations tend to know each other's situations and interests. An inside recommendation is a great tip.

Now Where Do I Go?

CONTACTS

Independent Sector
www.independentsector.org
Updates the hourly cost of volunteer time.

N.C. Center for Nonprofits
www.ncnonprofits.org
Helpful ideas and links.

www.fdncenter.org/learn/shortcourse/prop1.html
Proposal writing

nonprofit.miningco.com/msubgra.htm
Proposal writing

Grantsmanship Center
www.tgci.com

Association of Small Foundations
www.smallfoundations.org

BOOKS

The Foundation Center's Guide to Proposal Writing, 3rd Edition
By Jane C. Geever and Patricia McNeill

Secrets of Successful Grantsmanship: A Guerrilla Guide to Raising Money
By Susan L. Golden

Proposal Planning and Writing
By Jerry Griffith and Lynne E. Miner

Grantseeking: A Basic Step-by-Step Approach
By Lehman Zimmerman and Associates

Finding Funding: Grantwriting from Start to Finish Including Project Management and Internet Use
Edited by Ernest W. Brewer, Charles Achilles, Jay R. Fuhrimann, and Connie Hollingsworth

The Complete Guide to Getting a Grant: How to Turn Your Ideas into Dollars
By Laurie Blum

Creating a budget

what is a grant budget?

Just like any other balance sheet

Great, you've written your boilerplate grant proposal and included a basic budget summary. You're almost there! Depending on the complexity of your project, you may need to include a **project budget.** What's that? It's an accounting or list that breaks down the value of each and every item. How do you do that?

Well, first things first. A **budget** is a listing of expenses and income. A **balanced budget** means that when you subtract your expenses from your income, it equals $0. If you have never done a budget, don't panic. You can do it. Just take it one step at a time.

Start by going through your proposal, looking for all the goods

and services that you need money for, such as meeting space or a supervisor to oversee the project. These are considered **expenses**. Next, look for financial support that you already have, for example, money your project might have earned from selling raffle tickets, other grants you may have received, or **in-kind donations**—goods and services that are donated toward your project. (In-kind donations are critical to a grant budget; read more about them on page 66.) All this financial support is considered **revenue.**

Now grab your calculator. Add up your expenses. Then add up your income. The two numbers don't match, do they? Well, at this point, that's okay. They aren't supposed to. What will make them balance is the grant money you are requesting. That's why the grant money you are asking for from a foundation is called the **balance request.**

TIP: Divide your budget into key parts, such as staffing, facilities, and transportation, and ask several donors to fund a part of your project.

ASK THE EXPERTS

Is the project budget the same as the nonprofit sponsor's operating budget?

No, your project's budget is different from your nonprofit's operating budget. You need to include both in your grant proposal. Chances are some of the funding for your project will come from the operating budget of your nonprofit sponsor. For example, the operating budget usually lists the annual salary of the executive director and the project director. But in your project budget, list only the percentage of time that will be spent by the staff person on the project. For example, your project may require 30% of the executive director's time.

What if I want a lot of stuff to make the project special, but actually need less to get by?

Funders usually like to see that you have thought through the best-case scenario and the worst-case scenario. Your project budget should show the minimum amount necessary to do a good job. But feel free to attach a larger second budget, or add a footnote with the bigger figure, explaining what you'd do with more money.

Can I include administrative costs in the budget?

Sure! Most foundations expect 10% to 15% of your grant proposal budget to include administrative costs such as audits, office supplies, rent, utilities, and other similar expenses.

in-kind support

It's key to getting grants

Donors who give grant money like to see what other sources of support you have, such as grants from other donors. But they especially like to see that you have backing from your community. This backing can be anything from a large volunteer staff to donated goods from a local tech store. In grantland, this type of support is called **in-kind support**, and even though it's the giving of goods and services, it counts as income. Think of it as found money. In preparing your budget, you will need to put a price on every in-kind item you can think of.

Ask these questions to help you figure out your in-kind support.

■ **Are there aspects of your project that can piggyback on other projects that are already funded?** Perhaps you can use available space in your local school. Or perhaps you can use room in your nonprofit sponsor's headquarters. Assign a dollar amount next to these "free" items and list them as in-kind goods.

■ **Are there people who will volunteer their time and expertise?** Give each of those volunteers who will be working on the project an hourly rate, for example, $10 to $20 an hour for ticket takers, gift shop clerks, and event hosts (more for professionals such as lawyers and professors). Next, estimate the numbers of hours they will be working. The total amount will add to your in-kind support. (See page 67 for more on hourly rates.)

■ **Are there any donated goods on hand?** Think about all the things you will need, from office furniture to stationery. You may already have items left over from a previous project, such as stationery. If so, list them. Some donations may be new, for example, a bank that is renovating might give you used computers and office furniture. Put prices next to these goods and list the amount as in-kind support.

ASK THE EXPERTS

How can volunteers help my request for a grant?

Your request for a grant will score higher if you include volunteers as part of your plan. Foundations love to see community involvement for a project, and nearly all projects have volunteers who offer their time. Don't overlook this huge pool of support. Your job is to estimate the number of volunteers you will need, their level of work (some may be doing highly skilled work, such as bookkeeping, while others may be answering the phone). Then, put an hourly rate next to their work and estimate the hours they will be working.

What hourly rate do I put down for the volunteers?

Light clerical jobs such as phone answering and professional services such as tutoring don't have fixed pay scales. But you can find out what local businesses are paying for such tasks by calling a temporary employment agency or other business and just asking them, adding in the cost of benefits. If the volunteer task doesn't match a regular job, check similar jobs in want ads or on job-hunter sites. For professionals—for example, lawyers or accountants—who donate their services, ask them what they usually charge. (At **www.independentsector.org** under "research" and "dollar value of volunteer time," $16.05 was the estimated hourly average value of volunteer time in 2001, the latest available data.)

I was told I needed to show how we got some of our in-kind donations. Where do I put this information?

You can create a footnote. The footnote will explain which individual or organization donated the item. You can put this footnote in the relevant budget section or create a separate footnotes page and attach it to your budget. (See page 71 for a sample of footnotes.)

staff and consultants

Account for the people on the payroll

Some projects are simple and need only a few items for the budget. Others are more complicated, calling for salaried people to operate them. Some need to hire consultants, and still others require contract employees to make a project happen. Payroll and benefits, such as health insurance and pensions, are considered expenses and are often the single largest project expense. You need to list the titles and status (staff or freelance) of the key people your project needs.

Start with the staff—the folks already employed by the nonprofit organization that is sponsoring your grant. For example, if you are writing a grant to get money to help tutor children in your town, your local school will be your nonprofit sponsor. You will need to include the titles of the individuals who work at the school and will be involved in the tutoring project. Figure out what percentage of their time they will allocate to the project you are getting a grant for. For example, if the school librarian will be spending time overseeing the project to be funded, you need to figure out the percentage of time she will be committing to the project. Then you need to put that number against her annual salary and benefits. So if the librarian makes $50,000 a year with $10,000 in benefits and is committing 20% of her time to the project for 12 months, then in your budget you list her staff salary cost at $10,000 and the benefits at $2,000.

What if you need to hire staff? It's pretty much the same—you include their salary and benefits and note whether they will be working full- or part-time.

Consultants and other freelance helpers, such as writers and speakers, are considered contract employees. You need to note their hourly rate and the time they are committing to the project. Contract employees are usually not paid staff benefits such as health insurance. They are expected to provide their own.

ASK THE EXPERTS

What is the difference between project employees and contract employees?

Project employees are usually full-time hires who qualify for health insurance benefits. Contract employees, on the other hand, are essentially self-employed. They hire out their time or services and pay for their own benefits. Other contract employees may be on the payroll as part-time employees and have taxes and other payments deducted from their pay. In either case, there should be a written agreement specifying the number of hours the person will work, the rate of pay, the length of the contract, and any cancellation policies for either side.

We want to hire a consultant to help train our volunteer tutors. Her hourly rate is pretty expensive. Will that be bad for our grant?

Foundations often use government rates when paying for their own consultants and look for similar low rates when funding grants. If you really need this consultant, you should show that her rate is within the norm for her industry or profession. How? Get some kind of documentation that her rate is indeed the market rate and will be a more efficient use of time and money than hiring another full-time or part-time staff person. The consultant should be able to tell you whom to contact for this information. Then you can explain the rate in a footnote to the budget. You can also include three bids for a consultant and explain that you chose the most expensive because of her greater experience.

Will grant money cover training for staff and volunteers?

Sure. If staff training will be a major factor, you may want to enter it as a separate section in the budget. Just be careful; if too large a portion of the budget is required for training, you might be turned down. Reduce training needs by hiring consultants with the skills and experience needed to do the job.

facilities

How to itemize space and equipment

Will your project need its own space—an office, lab, storage space, or parking area? Will your project need to pay for this space? If so, be sure to list all connected expenses in your budget. The good news is that corporations in your area may be keen to provide in-kind donations of space and equipment. Another good idea is to put an ad in your local paper asking for donations of the specific equipment you need. You will be surprised by the offers you will get.

If you do find free space or equipment, give it a dollar value and list it in the in-kind section in your budget. You will want to provide a footnote naming the donor. The donor could be another foundation, a corporation, an individual, or your sponsoring nonprofit organization.

Note: Whether the space is paid for by the project or an in-kind donation, you need to factor in the amount of time you will be using it. If you will be using a certain space only part-time or for a few months full-time, the cost should reflect the amount of time it will be used. The same goes for other facilities expenses, such as heating, air conditioning, lighting, water, sewer, and telephones.

FIRST PERSON DISASTER STORY
A Simple Ad Made All the Difference

Our project required a hall to perform our student-directed theatrical productions. The fees to rent halls in our city were pretty high, and I was afraid donors would reject our grant when they saw the rental price. Sure enough, they did. A friend gave me a great idea to put an ad in the paper asking for donations of performance space. I got a call from the owner of an old factory who had a huge warehouse he could lend us for the season. With that item listed as an in-kind donation, I resubmitted our grant proposal, and we got our funding.

—Sarah T., Detroit, Michigan

Sample Facilities Budget

Here's a hypothetical budget for facilities needed for the Growing Great Readers project described in chapter 3. Note the footnotes at the bottom describing sources of in-kind support and donations.

	Expenses	In-Kind Support	Other Donations
FACILITIES			
Project Staff			
Office for director and secretary	$ 5,500		
Computer equipment for director and secretary			$ 1,200[1]
Office furnishings		$ 1,800 [2]	
Project Activities			
School cafeteria (after school and evenings) for tutoring and parent workshops		$ 15,000[3]	
Heating, air conditioning, lighting, and added security during after-hours use of school cafeteria	$ 6,000		
Total In-Kind Support and Other Donations		$ 18,000	
Total Facilities	$ 11,500		

Notes

[1] Funds for buying office computers and printer donated by Worthington Foundation

[2] In-kind donations of used office furnishings by First National Bank of Thursdon Hills

[3] In-kind donation of space part-time by Thursdon Hills Elementary School

other expenses

It's the small stuff
you really ought
to sweat

Many of the things necessary for a project's success don't appear under "personnel" or "facilities." These expenses go by other names, such as **nonpersonnel line items.** And that's a term that covers a multitude of miscellaneous expenditures, including transportation, lighting, postage, and stationery.

Basically, these expenses fall into the "other" category—but don't let the throwaway name fool you into thinking they're not important. All too often, grantwriters forget to include this type of expense in grant budgets, and consequently many projects run out of funds sooner than anticipated. So be wise and try to consider every expense the project may incur.

Some foundations will accept a line item in the budget for administrative costs to cover a multitude of smaller expenses such as supplies, copying, postage, bookkeeping, travel, and publications. Others want these listed. Certain foundations, especially corporations, allow a percentage (up to 10% of the grant in some cases) for "overhead."

Accounting By the Feds

Federal government grant applications recognize the importance of "other" expenses by using two budget categories: direct costs and indirect costs. Let's say a van is needed to deliver meals in a program for feeding the homebound elderly. The cost for the van and its operating expenses are considered direct costs. The cost of an award ceremony to honor volunteer drivers would be an indirect cost.

TIP: Expenses are based on the length of the project, from its projected start date until its completion date. If it's a multi-year project, you will need to include cost-of-living increases and project growth. Be sure to keep documentation for all expenses. You may need it to justify your spending to your grantmaker.

Make It a Collaborative Project

If you have several prospective donors who have common areas of interest, consider setting up a formal collaboration among them for the funding of your project. Donors generally like to be involved in collaborations because it takes the pressure off each one to fund an entire project. How do you propose such an arrangement? Send a letter of inquiry to each donor and call each one in a few weeks. But coordinating a collaborative project can be a little more time-consuming because it means that many more evaluation reports to file. This is a small thing, though, if it means your project is fully funded.

ASK THE EXPERTS

I have no idea how much some of the stuff we'll need for our project will cost. Can't we just guess?

Not a good idea. You will look inexperienced to prospective donors who happen to be knowledgeable about your field, and your grant may be rejected. Moreover, having to go back to ask for more, or failing to reach your objectives because of low budget estimates, can hurt your reputation in the donor community. It's smarter to take the time to get written estimates where possible. Or keep notes on how you came up with your estimates. Then, if you have to go back to a donor for more money you can explain what changed. Donors appreciate it when you gather and offer good records and information.

What if we make an error in our budget and run out of money before our project is completed?

That happens. Don't panic. Once your grant is accepted, you will be making monthly or quarterly reports to the donor that should include a regular budgetary update. If there is a shortfall, don't wait for your next scheduled report. Go to the donor immediately. The funder may be able to help you by allocating extra funds or suggesting where else you might apply.

revenue

Funding you already have

This usually comes as a surprise to first time grantwriters: You already have money on hand. Really? Where? All the in-kind donations you have are considered **revenue** (money that was donated). Also, if you have gotten any other grants for this project, they are considered revenue. On your budget, list donors and their committed funds you are expecting. Another source of revenue is fund-raising. This could be anything from membership dues to a special event that usually takes in a certain

amount—for example, an annual professional/amateur sports event that typically raises $10,000 for your particular nonprofit. Don't be shy about listing as many sources of revenue as you can. The more you show, the more viable your organization appears.

But what if your project is about making money? What if, for example, you need money to put on a play for which you intend to charge admission? What then? That money has to go toward a nonprofit cause, namely your project. And that is what a lot of funders want to see happen. Whenever possible, the goal is to create a self-funding project. The money you make from that play, for instance, will be listed as revenue in your budget for next year. And should you need to apply for a grant the following year, the donor will see when you list the ticket revenue and fund-raising revenue in your budget that you are on your way toward funding your own projects.

ASK THE EXPERTS

What if the project attracts a lot more funding from donors than we expected in the budget?

That's good news. However, if your project was a one-time thing, be prepared to hand over some or all of the grant money you got. At the same time, foundation program officers love to hear that your program attracted more money than expected. Tell them about your plans for spending the extra money. If your project is an ongoing one, share the good news with your funder and ask if you may apply the funds to next year's project or to do all those extra things you wanted to do this year. The program officer is likely to say yes or may offer other suggestions for spending the money.

What if the grant we are applying for offers only a specific amount and our request is more than that amount?

A number of funders give grants in set amounts, such as $5,000 or $10,000, and no more. If your request is more than that amount, you have two choices: Consider applying to additional donors for the difference and list them in your budget, or scale down your budget so it fits the amount the donor is giving. (This is why tailoring your grant proposal to fit the donor's aims is critical. For more on this, see chapter 8.) Except for government grants, it's a good idea to limit your request to 50% of your project's budget. Potential funders like to see that you are asking for grants from other organizations and using some of your other resources for funding the project.

your budget request

What you need from the donor

You are almost done! You've gotten your expenses together and you listed any donations and revenues you may have. Great! Now what? You are just one calculation away from determining how much money to ask for from a funder. Subtract your revenues from your expenses and you should get the magic number. This number is your **balance request,** what you want donors to supply with grants.

Will one foundation spring for everything you requested? Not likely. Donors like to be part of projects that list community support and other grants or requests for other grants. How many other donors might you have to ask for funds? The best way to know is to check the records of the foundation to which you're applying (see page 100). If they're giving out money to other organizations in similar amounts, you may get what you request. If your organization is new, you may get less. If their donations are smaller than what you need, scale back your request. For example, ask for the cost of facilities or the salaries of major personnel. If you decide to ask for smaller amounts from several donors with modest donation records, explain what you're doing so each donor will know exactly how much you're requesting from them and others. *Donors expect you to look for money from several funders and may even direct you to others.*

When a donor has a record of giving amounts large enough to address your entire request, you can appeal for the full amount in your cover letter (see page 158) and in the proposal's summary as well. You might want to offer to name the program after the donor. It often works!

SK THE EXPERTS

What are the most common errors people make when drawing up a grant budget?

The most common mistake is underestimating costs. It's a problem that plagues both the nonprofit and the for-profit world. Another common error is underestimating in-kind donations. To help combat these mistakes, be sure to have your budget reviewed by a number of people: the executive director and treasurer of the nonprofit that is sponsoring your project, and any financial contacts you have in the for-profit world.

TIP: When your accountant is preparing the annual audit for your nonprofit organization or your nonprofit sponsor, ask for additional originals up front. They are usually cheaper when done all at once. Then, you'll have them when you need to submit them with grant proposals. Most foundations will not accept a photocopy of your audit. They want to see the auditor's original signature, usually in blue ink.

Budget Narrative

Some donors want a written version of your numerical budget. This is called a budget narrative, and it's where you describe expense items in detail. So instead of a simple listing (such as "Project director, $4,500"), you need to write out the job description to back up the cost.

a sample budget

Getting to the bottom line

Here is a budget format that would be appropriate for many donors. But always follow the guidelines from the individual funder when compiling your budget.

	Expenses	In-Kind Support and Other Donations
PERSONNEL		
Project Staff		
Project Director	$ 55,000	
Project Secretary	$ 14,100	
Thursdon Hills Elementary School staff		
Principal	$ 4,750	
Two first-grade teachers coordinating		
with Project Director	$ 4,140	
Staff salaries	$ 77,990	
Benefits packages (18%)	$ 14,040	
TOTAL STAFF	$ 92,030	
Consultants		
Reading Consultant	$ 10,000 [1]*	
Promotion Director	$ 5,000	
TOTAL CONSULTANTS	$ 15,000	
Volunteers		
Tutors		$ 112,800 [2]*
TOTAL PERSONNEL	$107,030	$ 112,800

*See Notes on page 79.

	Expenses	In-Kind Support and Other Donations
FACILITIES		
Offices		
Office for director and secretary	$ 5,500	
Computer equipment for director and secretary		$ 1,200[3]
Office furnishings		$ 1,800[4]
Activity Space		
School cafeteria, afterschool and evenings for tutoring and parent workshops		$ 15,000[5]
Heating, air conditioning, lighting, and added security during after-hours use of school cafeteria	$ 6,000	
TOTAL FACILITIES	$ 11,500	$ 18,000
OTHER EXPENSES		
Office supplies	$ 1,000	
Estimated phone and utilities	$ 1,220	
Bus fare for volunteer tutors		$ 9,000[6]
Administrative expenses	$ 2,000	
TOTAL OTHER	$ 4,220	$ 9,000
TOTAL EXPENSES	$122,750	
TOTAL IN-KIND SUPPORT AND OTHER DONATIONS		$ 139,800

BUDGET TOTAL	$ 262,550
Minus total in-kind support and other donations	$ 139,800

Contributions Required $ 122,750

This is how much money you need to ask for from various donors.

Notes

(1) The consultant will advise the teachers and director Aug.–Nov.; and evaluate the project during June

(2) In-kind support from volunteers among residents at Thursdon Hills Retirement Community

(3) Funds for buying office computers and printer donated by the Worthington Foundation

(4) In-kind donations of used office furnishings by First National Bank of Thursdon Hills

(5) In-kind donation of space part-time by Thursdon Hills Elementary School

(6) In-kind donation of bus passes by Thursdon Hills Township

now what do I do?

Answers to common questions

These operating budgets seem pretty elaborate. Do all budgets have to be this long?

No. Often a simple project has a one- or two-category budget. For instance, if you are asking for new computers for your school, you might put together a budget that just lists the hardware, the software, the shipping and installation, and the training costs. Or say your library has lost its funding for new books this year; you might ask for enough money to allow the librarian to buy the customary number of books. In that case, you might not even need a separate budget, since the total amount would be going to one item, the cost of the books. The more complicated the project, the more complex the budget.

I am preparing a budget for a two-year project. Can I show an increase in salaries to accommodate the cost-of-living increase for the second year?

Yes, as a separate line item. It should be the percentage increase based on the listed salary for the current year. You will also want to include any increase for rent that might be imposed. If there are several such items, they could be listed in a separate section called "Second-Year Expenses."

What other financial information do I need to include with my proposal?

Most prospective donors request:

1. The most recent audited financial statement of your sponsoring organization.
2. A copy of at least one year's annual budget for the sponsoring organization.
3. A copy of the organization's most recent 501(c)3 letter from the IRS.
4. A list of key personnel and the board of directors.
5. Sometimes an IRS Form 990PF.

I hear it's important to ask several donors for funding. How do I divide my request between the five donors I've selected?

You can ask each donor to fund a part of your project. Look at the amounts of past grants of each of the donors. If a donor usually gives grants of $5,000 to $10,000, request a similar amount. If a donor usually gives grants of $100,000 or more, you can comfortably ask for that amount. Match your request with the relative assets of the foundation. For example, don't ask a huge foundation for only $5,000 if it has a history of giving $300,000.

Now Where Do I Go?

CONTACTS

National Network of Grantmakers
www. nng.org
Find a common grant application with an appended
budget that you can use as you create your budget.

Foundation Center sample budgets
fdncenter.org/learn/faqs/samplebudget.html

Foundation Center Learning Lab
fdncenter.org/learn/shortcourse/prop1.html

Foundation Center
fdncenter.org/learn/
Select: Proposal Budgeting Basics

Sample Budget Forms

Nonprofit Guides
www.npguides.org/index.html

Bush Foundation
www.bushfoundation.org/apply/
ProgGrantSampleBudget.htm

Cleveland Foundation
www.clevelandfoundation.org/
page1679.cfm

BOOKS

**The Budget-Building Book for Nonprofits: A
Step-by-Step Guide for Managers and Boards**
By Murray Dropkin and Bill LaTouche

**The Foundation Center's Guide to Proposal
Writing, 3rd Edition**
By Jane C. Geever and Patricia McNeill

**A Nonprofit Organization
Operating Manual: Planning
for Survival and Growth**
By Arnold J. Olenick and Philip R. Olenick

Grant Seeker's Budget Toolkit
By James A. Quick and Cheryl C. New

Finding private donors

narrowing the search

Know what to look for before you start looking

You've got your project, budget, and proposal. You're now ready to get a donor. Great, but before you rush your proposal to the first good-looking foundation you find, consider this: Who's most likely to actually give you the funds? The best candidate is a foundation with a mission that matches your project. The closer the match, the more likely the donor is to consider your request. If your grant is for a project to feed the homeless in your community, look for a donor that's dedicated to reducing poverty in your community. And pass over donors dedicated to, say, overseas famine relief.

Once you have found your mission match, look to see if there are any **restrictions.** Most restrictions deal with geography and demographics—the donor will only fund projects in a specific state or town or for a specific group of people such as homeless women, veterans, or blind students.

FIRST PERSON DISASTER STORY
Mission Drift

I was pretty sure I had found the perfect foundation to fund our program. Their mission statement was fairly similar to ours except where we were looking to solve a number of social issues with practical intervention, they were keen on providing academic analysis of these problems. I rewrote our proposal with their mission in mind and added a couple of professors to the project. We got the grant, but the professors required a lot of hand-holding and it took us off target from our original mission. I realize now how important it is to stay on track with the mission.

—Andy T., Tacoma, Washington

Other restrictions apply to the nature of the grants themselves. Some foundations will not consider anything under $50,000, and others can't exceed $5,000. Still others have restrictions about the types of grants they give out (see page 18). For example, some funders will give money for operating grants, while others will fund only project grants. Government grants also have restrictions. (For information on government grants, see chapter 6.)

STEP BY STEP
Smart research

Before you start your research, get a clear idea of the kind of funding you need. Fill out a worksheet with the answers to these questions to help you focus your research.

1. What type of grant do you want?
(Start-up, program, or other type. See page 18 for details.)

2. Is there an overall mission to your project?
(You want to match your mission to a funder's mission statement.)

3. What categories does the project fit in?
(Pick as many as possible. For a project to teach soccer to underprivileged children, look for donors focused on recreation, children's health, mental health, and sports.)

4. What specific group of people will the project help?

5. Where is it located?

6. How much money do you need?

7. When is the grant money needed?
(Some funders take six months to review grants; others conduct monthly reviews.)

researching potential donors

Web sites, libraries, and directories

You know what your project needs and you're ready to go after it. But where do you go to find the names of potential donors? Why, where the information is, of course—at your local public library and online with your home computer.

At the library, head for the reference section and ask for the directories of philanthropic organizations. These large tomes list the three main types of funders—**foundations, corporate funders,** and **government agencies.** For corporate funding, for example, check out the *National Directory of Corporate Giving.* Or check out directories by subject. If you're looking to fund your community theater, go for directories on the arts. Or pick the best match for your project from donor directories devoted to health, environment, religion, science, women's issues, and other topics. For example, in *Grants for Children and Youth,* you'll find 21,820 grants of $10,000 or more, categorized by state, foundation name, address, and the restrictions of each donor.

The Internet is another good starting point, especially the Web site for the Foundation Center. This site is a repository for all things related to grants (except government-sponsored grants, which you can learn about in chapter 6). On the Internet, go to the Foundation Center at **www.fdncenter.org**. Other good donor research sites include **www.fundsnetservices.com**, **www.ncnonprofits.org**, and **www.nonprofits.org**.

The big advantage to Web sites is that you can narrow down donor lists using **keywords** (descriptive words that you type into an Internet search engine) that are relevant to your project. The more keywords you use, the more relevant matches you'll get.

Want to Hire a Researcher to Do All This for You?

Does this research sound like too much work? Then get a pro to do it for you. Post your project as a temp job at a relevant Web site, such as the Association of Fundraising Professionals, the Association of Professional Researchers for Advancement, the Foundation Center, and the sites of related organizations. Web site addresses appear on page 103.

TIP: Look in your files. Don't forget previous donors. Ask long-time volunteers; they may recall past supporters that aren't in your files.

Your Prospective Donor Worksheet

You are going to be inundated with information. Don't let it overwhelm you—get organized before you start your search. Make a form like this one to keep track of the specifics about each potential donor. Fill out the form for each prospective donor you come across. Later, use the forms to pick the most likely donor candidates.

DONOR WORKSHEET

Name of organization _____

Address _____

_____

Contact names _____

E-mail address _____

Contact numbers _____

Types of grants
(project, restricted, fellowship, etc.) _____

Geographic restrictions _____

Population restrictions _____

Subjects of interest _____

_____

Amount of annual giving _____

Funding guidelines _____

_____

Examples of past donations _____

Deadlines _____

foundations

They have one
purpose: to make
donations to
worthy causes

As you look through directories of donors, one word keeps cropping up: foundations. And because there are about 56,000 foundations in the United States that give away some $30 billion a year in grants, it's important for you to know a thing or two about them.

Foundations are legal entities designed to give a formal structure to philanthropic giving. Most are **independent foundations**—that is, they are set up by private individuals or families who put a portion of their money toward philanthropic work.

Corporations form another big portion of the philanthropic world through their **corporate foundations** (see page 94). The last major category is **community** or **public foundations.** These focus on a specific geographic area and are funded by local sources.

As you begin your search, you will find foundations that match your project. When you do, write down the contact information on your donor worksheets. Then contact those foundations and get some more information about them. Here's what you should request.

Annual reports   Many foundations issue annual reports describing their charitable giving for the year. These reports also detail guidelines used for evaluating proposals. You usually can obtain a copy by calling the foundation's office or ordering one online.

Brochures   Foundations without elaborate annual reports or Web sites will often send you leaflets or brochures at your request outlining how they choose recipients and specifying guidelines for completing proposal submissions.

Applications   Some have formal applications and some don't.

If you are planning to call a foundation for more than one of these items, be sure to make all requests in one phone call.

At right, a sample entry from the 2002 edition of The Foundation Directory shows contacts, past grants, and other information you need to select potential donors.

Entry number

7823
The Sisler McFawn Foundation

Street address

P.O. Box 149
Akron, OH 44309-0149 (330) 849-8887

Person to whom inquiries should be addressed

Contact: Charlotte M. Stanley, Grants Mgr.
FAX: (330) 996-6215

Establishment data

Trust established in 1959 in OH.
Donor(s): Lois Sisler McFawn.‡
Foundation type: Independent
Financial data (yr. ended 12/31/00): Assets, $22,441,814 (M); expenditures, $1,631,265; qualifying distributions, $1,435,428; giving activities include $1,445,619 for 86 grants (high: $300,000; low: $1,500).

Year-end date of accounting period

Assets at market value (M) or ledger value (L)

Total expenditures figure

Amount and number of grants paid

Separate information on amount and number of employee matching gifts, grants to individuals, or loans

Areas of foundation giving

Purpose and activities: Giving primarily for education, social services, and for special needs populations such as the elderly, children from disadvantaged families, and the disabled.
Fields of interest: Education; health care; human services; children & youth, services; disabled; aging; economically disadvantaged.

Types of grants and other types of support

Types of support: General/operating support; continuing support; annual campaigns; capital campaigns; building/renovation; equipment; endowments; program development; seed money; curriculum development; scholarship funds; matching/challenge support.

Limitations: Giving primarily in Summit County, OH. No support for churches. No grants to individuals, or for computer equipment; no loans.

Specific limitations on foundation giving by geographic area, subject focus, or types of support

Printed material available from the foundation

Publications: Application guidelines, grants list.
Application information: Application form not required.

Application information

Initial approach: Full proposal
Copies of proposal: 1
Deadline(s): 45 days prior to board meeting; Mar. 15, July 15, and Oct. 15
Board meeting date(s): 1st week of May, Sept., and Dec.
Final notification: Within 3 weeks of board meeting

Distribution Committee: Jon V. Heider, Pres.; H. Peter Burg, Michael J. Connor, Howard L. Flood, Patricia A. Kemph, John L. Macso, Justin T. Rogers, Jr.
Trustee: Key Trust Co. of Ohio, N.A.
Number of staff: 1 part-time professional.
EIN: 346508111

Officers and Trustees or other governing bodies

IRS Identification Number

Selected grants

Selected grants: The following grants were reported in 1999.
$100,000 to Summit Education Initiative, Akron, OH.
$60,000 to Ohio Foundation of Independent Colleges, Columbus, OH.
$55,000 to Greater Akron Musical Association, Akron, OH.
$50,000 to University of Akron, Akron, OH.
$50,000 to YMCA, Akron Metropolitan Board, Akron, OH.
$35,000 to United Way of Summit County, Akron, OH.
$30,000 to Hiram College, Hiram, OH.
$30,000 to Summit Academy Community School for Alternative Learners, Akron, OH.
$22,500 to United Disability Services, Akron, OH.
$18,000 to Community Support Services, Brookfield, IL.

Symbols

▼ Identifies foundations for which in-depth descriptions have been prepared for inclusion in the Foundation Center's *Foundation 1000.*

✧ Indicates entries prepared or updated by Center staff from public records.

☆ Indicates foundations that did not appear in previous edition.

‡ Indicates individual is deceased.
(L) Ledger value of assets.
(M) Market value of assets.
* Officer is also a trustee or director.
+ indicates an unspecified number of grants.

the Foundation Center

A library of foundations

If the grant world seems a bit overwhelming, be grateful you weren't doing this 50 years ago. Back then, there was no central repository of grant data. That's why the heads of several leading philanthropic foundations got together and established the Foundation Center.

Based in its headquarters in New York City, the Foundation Center publishes dozens of helpful directories listing funding sources. Here are some of its resource guides that you might find handy.

- **The Foundation Directory** This multivolume set offers in-depth information on over 56,000 private and community foundations.

- **National Directory of Corporate Giving** This directory profiles more than 3,300 corporate donors.

- **Foundation Grants to Individuals** This publication lists more than 4,300 donors focused on personal grants. (See chapter 7.)

- **National Guides** This series of guides covers around 8,000 donors in different categories, including the *National Guide to Funding in Religion*, and titles in arts and culture, AIDS, and higher education.

- **Regional directories** The Foundation Center offers directories for several states. A title like *New York State Foundations* lists over 7,000 foundations located in New York.

The Foundation Center also has offices in Washington, D.C., San Francisco, Cleveland, and Atlanta and strong ties with 200 major libraries around the country. So somewhere near you, you can get the information you need—and you will probably find librarians and other helpful folks to make your donor search easier.

ASK THE EXPERTS

How do I find the library nearest to me that's affiliated with the Foundation Center?

To find a Foundation Center–affiliated library, write to the Foundation Center, 79 Fifth Avenue, New York, NY 10003-3076; call 212-620-4230 or 800-424-9836; or check the Web site at **www.fdncenter.org**.

Can I buy their books on CD?

Yes. The Foundation Center has converted some of its books into CD's, but they are pricey. The CD with data for the largest 10,000 foundations costs $295, and the one with the largest 20,000 foundations costs $495. Good news: CDs can be used free of charge in Foundation Center libraries.

Does the Foundation Center provide any training in the grant-seeking process?

Yes, it does. Foundation Center courses cover many of the crucial subject areas, including writing grant proposals, assembling budgets, researching prospective donors, and reading tax forms. Some courses are also available online at the Foundation Center Web site. In addition, the center hosts day-long seminars in many locations around the country. The two most popular topics are its Proposal Writing Seminar and Grantseeking on the Web ($195 each). See the center's Web site for dates and locations.

the Foundation Center online

Your search just got easier

Lucky you! You're looking for a grant in the Internet Age. More grants—and tips on how to apply for them—arrive online every day. Using a computer and a connection to the World Wide Web will save you time and help you search for opportunities faster than scanning a hefty volume at the public library.

But if you don't have a computer at home or work, your library should still be your first stop because many offer computers for public use.

Plan to spend your first visit online just browsing, much the way you might the first time you go out house hunting. You will get ideas, narrow the field, and come away with a list of wonderful choices.

First, go to the Foundation Center at **www.fdncenter.org**. Most of the good stuff is reserved for subscribers paying about $20 a month and up, but you can find links and basic descriptions of more than 67,000 donors by clicking on the Foundation Finder link, the Grantmaker Web sites link, and others listed under Finding Funders.

In the Foundation Finder, you'll find alphabetical lists of foundations broken down into four categories—private foundations, corporate grantmakers, grantmaking public charities, and community foundations. You'll see the links to the categories on the left side of the Web page—click on one and you'll find the pages you need to research further.

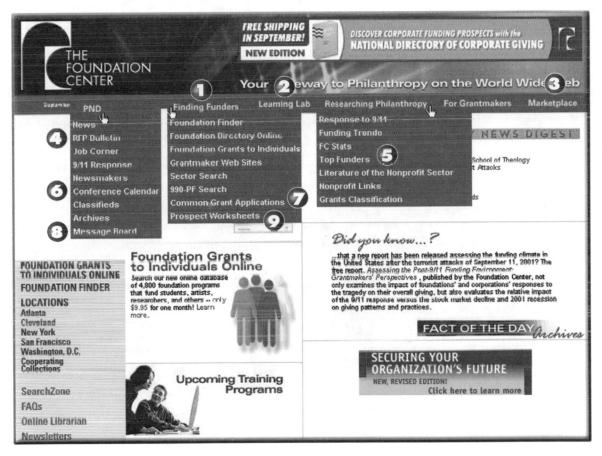

You can look for donors and research grants at the Foundation Center Web site.

Here is a sample of what you'll find:

1. Free access to a broad list of grants

2. Free proposal-writing tips

3. Proposal-writing seminars

4. New grant opportunities, known as RFP's (Requests for Proposals)

5. Top 100 funders by asset size

6. Conference calendar

7. Common grant application forms

8. Message boards

9. Prospect worksheets

corporations

The friendly face of capitalism

Many major corporations make donations to good causes. Some have their own nonprofit foundations that work just like nonprofit foundations funded by private sources. You can research their giving in a similar way. By law, corporations cannot seek direct benefits from such donations, and their giving may often be anonymous.

But there's another way in which corporations give to worthy causes. It's from funds taken out of their operating budgets, a method known as **direct corporate giving.** These gifts seem like investments in public relations, but the results are still good because the money goes to real charities. Corporate giving is typ-

ically concentrated in the community where the corporation is located. This is to make sure that donations benefit the com-pany's employees and customers. But giving is not limited to the national headquarters. Regional offices are often allowed to make donations to worthy causes, too. Any corporation with offices located in your area may be a good prospective donor for your project.

If you think a direct corporate gift is possible, seek out the corporation's marketing director, public relations director, or advertising agency. Call the company to find out to whom you should address your application.

Corporate Gifts Out of the Box

In-kind donations This kind of giving is a specialty of corporations, whether they're Fortune 500 companies or simple mom-and-pop stores. Instead of money, companies offer to supply goods to assist your project. Furnishings, computers, medicine, food, even empty offices are just a few possible in-kind benefits you might want to request. The type of assistance often depends on the products the company produces. Consider the equipment your project will require, then look for a local corporation or retail business as a possible source.

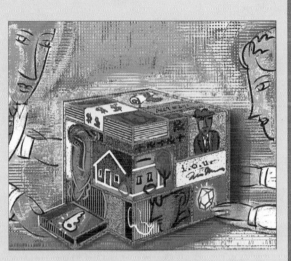

Technical assistance Many corporations offer their employees' time to philanthropic causes. For example, an after-school tutoring program might need advice on the best way to maintain their buses. Mechanics employed by a local company may spend an afternoon a week to help solve mechanical problems.

ASK THE EXPERTS

Will I lose a grant because we're not the only food pantry?

No. Mention the others in your proposal. Funders want to know that you know who else is meeting the need in your community. They also love collaboration. For example: "The nearest food pantry is 10 blocks away. They reached capacity serving 1,000 people a month. We propose to serve an additional 1,000 and will purchase food in bulk with the other existing program."

individual donors

The next time you go to a play or concert, look in the back of your program. Chances are there's a list of patrons who've given money to the arts organization sponsoring the performance. Donor names are often listed in several categories depending on the amount each person has given.

The ones at the top—donors of large sums of money—are usually exceptionally wealthy individuals. If they learn about your project and find it interesting, they may fund part of it by simply writing you a check.

Wealthy donors are not required by law to make their donations public, as foundations are. So how do you find out about their interests and assets? There are resources that will help you locate personal and professional information, such as newspaper archive searches, corporate officer listings (such as those at Hoovers Web site, **www.hoovers.com**), and plain old Web searches. Enter the name of an individual along with keywords such as "donation." For example, if you go to **www.google.com** and enter the name "Ima Richman" in quotation marks, followed by "donation," you'll probably find references to donations made by Ima Richman.

What should you look for? An address, or employment information—especially if the person is an officer or board member of a business. You may also be able to identify previous donations to other causes that might be related to yours. Biographical information, especially from newspaper and magazine articles, can tell you about personal interests, school affiliations, assets, and income, along with contact information.

STEP BY STEP

Checklist to see if an individual is a prospective donor

1. Does the individual have any corporate connections? If she is an officer or board member of a corporation, the nature of the company's business could indicate some of her interests.

2. What assets does he have? If he is a corporate executive, look at the company's **10-K** (quarterly financial filings that list large amounts of stock owned by corporate officers as well as their salaries). Also, check out what real estate has been selling for in his neighborhood. The prices can sometimes indicate how wealthy he might be.

3. What is his educational background? If he went to high school or college in the area where your project will be operating, or if his studies were in an area related to your project, he might want to contribute.

4. Does she donate to causes similar to yours? Is she listed as a donor for other nonprofit groups? Are the goals and missions of those groups related to the goals and mission of your project?

5. What are his hobbies and social interests? Does he spend his time doing volunteer work that relates to your proposal in some way? Or does he indulge in other pastimes that are related?

6. Are there family connections? If her parent or spouse has been interested in a certain philanthropy, she may share that interest. In the case of medical research projects, if a family member is suffering from a disease, it may prompt her to donate funds to study that disease or to help others who have it.

annual reports

You can learn a lot about a foundation from its **annual report.** In fact, this yearly record of an organization's achievements and financial statements can be a gold mine. Grant seekers can uncover the names of directors or trustees and find out their interests and talents from the committees they serve on. You can usually learn how much grant money they gave out—and often who the lucky recipients were or what they did with the award. (See page 100 for more.)

The report also usually includes the donor's **mission statement** (a brief, eloquent summary of the organization's purpose—for example, "to enhance the quality of life in XYZ City"), which will help you decide if your project fits in with its mission. In the donor's history, you may learn details that may match those of your project and that you can use when tailoring your proposal. (Find more on how to tailor your proposal in chapter 8.)

And if you're struggling for the right tone for your proposal, you can take your cues from the annual report. The more you mirror the donor and the other projects the donor has funded, the more likely it is that you will be next in line. In this case, imitation is not only the highest form of flattery but also the best route to getting a grant.

Sample Mission Statement

" The Scripps Howard Foundation strives to advance the cause of a free press through support of excellence in journalism, quality journalism education, and professional development. The foundation helps build healthy communities and improve the quality of life through support of sound educational programs, strong families, vital social services, enriching arts and culture, and inclusive civic affairs, with a special commitment to the communities in which the company does business. **"**

At right, useful elements of an annual report

1. Past grants
2. Potential contacts
3. Mission statement
4. History

Discretionary Grants

AMERICA'S PROMISE: THE ALLIANCE FOR YOUTH,
Alexandria, VA

FOR STRATEGIC PLANNING, $25,000

BROOKLYN PUBLIC LIBRARY, *Brooklyn, NY*

TOWARD THE EXPANSION OF EARLY CHILDHOOD
PROGRAMS TO PROMOTE READING, $25,000

CHILD CARE ACTION CAMPAIGN, *New York, NY*

TOWARD PLANNING A CAMPAIGN ON THE IMPORTANCE
CHILDHOOD LITERACY FOR CHILD CARE AND
TORS, $25,000

Committee on Trustees

Planning and Finance Committee

mission statement

Carnegie Corporation of New York was created by Andrew Carnegie in 1911 to promote "the advancement and diffusion of knowledge and understanding." Under Carnegie's will, grants must benefit the people of the United States, although up to 7.4 percent of the funds may be used for the same purpose in countries that are or have been members of the British Commonwealth, with a current emphasis on sub-Saharan Africa. As a grantmaking foundation the Corporation seeks to carry out Carnegie's vision of philanthropy, which he said should aim "to do real and permanent good in this world."

Some Reflections on the Historic Roots, Evolution and Future of American Phil

In its 1919 obituary for Andrew Carnegie, the *New York Sun* called him the of *Triumphant Democracy*," referring to Carnegie's own book on America. it gloated over statistical evidence of the young democracy's success, and in defe readers, Carnegie coated "the wholesome medicine of facts in the sweetest and

Source: Carnegie Corp. of New York 1999 and 2000 annual reports

990-PF's

The inside giving track

Great, you've found a few potential donors. You've gotten their annual reports, and found what seems to be a really good match. But what if nowhere in the reports does it say to whom the donor gave money in the past?

Surely, you say, you could find this out only by examining the IRS forms filed by the donor. And you'd be right. The good news is, you can look at the returned forms. Nonprofit groups are required to list the dollar amount and recipient of every grant they give in their annual filings. And these forms, called **990s** (for private foundations, it's form **990-PF**), are available to the public.

You can contact the public affairs department at your local IRS office and ask for the 990-PF forms of the foundations you're considering for requests. In some cases, you can uncover a foundation's 990-PF on the Web at **www.grantsmart.org**, **www.guide star.org**, and **www.fndncenter.org**. From the Grantsmart home page, click the Search link. This gives you access to search the database for more than 60,000 private foundations that file a 990-PF.

The more you know about how much and to whom a donor has given, the more you can gauge your project's chances of receiving money and how much to request.

Shorten your research by getting the 990 of nonprofits similar to yours. The forms will reveal the amounts of grant money the groups have *received* and from whom. Incorporate that list of donors into your list of potential donors.

Here's what to look for in donor tax returns, for example, the Target Foundation return at right.

1. **Name, address, and phone number**
2. **Recipients of past grants, purpose, and amount**
3. **Attachments: more past grant listings**

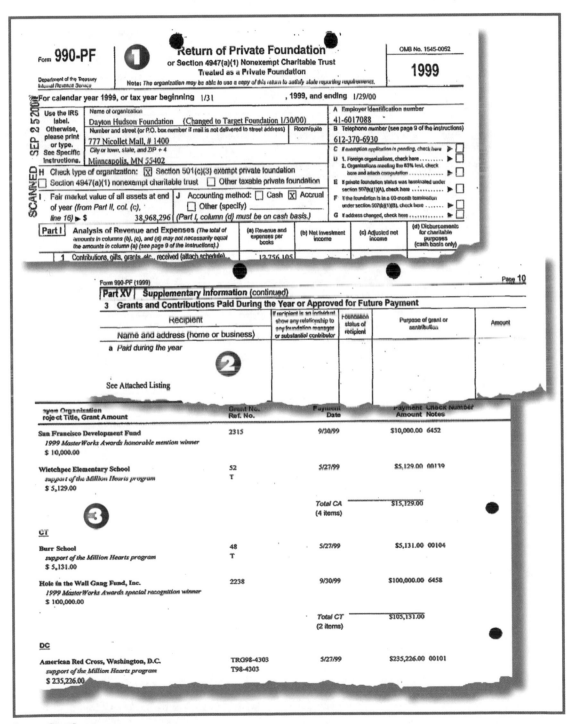

now what do I do?

Answers to common questions

Are there any clues that a foundation is not a good prospect?

If a foundation gives only one or two gifts annually, its funds may come from a single individual and go to predetermined recipients. If the gifts are very small each year, the donor may not have enough assets to give you much help. If giving is restricted to a specific type of grant, say project grants, and you need an operating grant, strike the foundation from your prospect list.

One listing in one of the Foundation Center's directories said, "No unsolicited applications accepted." Should I forget about them even though they've been funding projects similar to mine?

This may mean that the foundation counts on nominations from a committee it appoints to suggest grant recipients. But sometimes, this just means all the funds are allocated for the year, so keep it on your list for now. When you're ready to contact your potential list of donors (see page 86), you may want to make a polite inquiry and tell them about your project. But tread cautiously to avoid seeming pushy or ignorant.

Does it matter to donors who the recipients of program benefits are?

Sometimes. Say you need $50,000 for a tutoring program for disadvantaged children in a large city. A funder who is giving grants of $2,000 for soccer balls used at a private school in a wealthy suburb might not be interested in giving awards as large as the one you need. Plus, even though both programs are for after-school programs, they serve different demographics.

How can I judge if a foundation's grants are a close match to the one I'm seeking?

If the areas of interest are similar, then look for specifics. You both may have an interest in education. Check to see if the donor supports math projects like yours. If yes, you have a good chance. But if your program is for first-graders and the donor gives only to college projects, look for another donor that is a closer fit.

Are there any grant message boards that I can access to answer some basic questions I have?

Yes. Go to the Foundation Center's Web site at **www.fdncenter.org** or to CharityChannel at **www.charitychannel.org**. Look for links to click on such as

Community, Forums, or Message Boards. On CharityChannel, you can click Forums, a collection of more than 30 message boards on a variety of topics, including grants. On the grants page, click on Control Panel to get to the archives, where you can then select each month's grants. "Search the archives" to find this month's current messages about grants.

I am writing a grant for my daughter's preschool. They got a grant in the past from two foundations. What are the odds that those two foundations will help out again?

Very good. That's why all previous donors should be tops on your list. Since they have given in the past, it is clear your goals are a close fit with theirs.

Now Where Do I Go?

CONTACTS

GrantSmart
www.grantsmart.org
Find donor tax returns.

Foundation Center's Online Librarian
www.fdncenter.org
Look for the Learning Lab's Online Librarian.

Council on Foundations
www.cof.org

FC SEARCH: The Foundation Center's Database on CD-ROM 4.0

Association of Fundraising Professionals
www.afpnet.org

Association of Professional Researchers for Advancement
www.aprahome.org
Fund-raisers who specialize in research.

Association of Small Foundations
www.smallfoundations.org

BOOKS

National Directory of Nonprofit Organizations
Taft Group

Corporate Giving Directory 2002
Taft Group (Also see other Taft directories.)

Guide to U.S. Foundations
Foundation Center

National Guide to Funding in Aging
Foundation Center (Also see other Foundation Center Directories.)

The Foundation Center's Guide to Grantseeking on the Web

The Foundation Center's User-Friendly Guide: A Grantseeker's Guide to Resources, 4th Edition

finding government funders

government grants

Your tax dollars might come back to help your project

The government gives away millions in grants every year. There are so many that it takes a 1,500-page book, *The Catalog of Federal Domestic Assistance,* to list them—and it doesn't even include federal grants for the Corporation for Public Broadcasting and the National Institutes of Health. You can buy the book, but it is so unwieldy that it is sold unbound, so you may want to use the copy in your local library instead. But take along a magnifying glass and your most persistent manner. The type is tiny, and the pages are so thin you can almost see through them. Fortunately, the catalog is on the Internet (**www.cfda.gov**), which can make searching it somewhat easier.

There is one drawback to applying for a government grant. Even if your grant proposal is approved by a state or federal agency, you may wait in vain to receive a check. The reason is, a state legislature or Congress may not have allocated enough funds to cover all the grants that are approved. This means that the hours of work you have invested in filling out the lengthy government forms may not pay off after all.

If that happens, ask your legislator to look into the matter for you; yours may be one of the grants that are actually funded. Seeking a state grant may be easier than seeking a federal grant. You might find you are able to obtain support from a state representative or senator more readily than you could get it from a U.S. senator or representative.

On rare occasions, legislators might even be able to influence the outcome of grant proposals in various government agencies, but don't count on that. Government agencies generally use a committee of experts in your field to review your grant proposal. This process is called **peer review**. These experts take pride in their independent status, and they are not likely to be open to political influence.

ASK THE EXPERTS

How much money can I ask for from a federal grant? I see that some of the grants awarded are large.

The key to a successful government application is cost-effectiveness. Asking for a large amount of money is no problem if your project will serve a large number of people in your community. The cost-per-participant is what counts. Some government grant descriptions may even suggest a maximum allowable cost-per-participant. Your budget could come close to that amount but not exceed it.

How can I get information about grants given by the state?

The Internet is the easiest place to begin your hunt. Simply type your state's name in your browser's search window and add the words "government grants." Hundreds of sites will come up, which you will have to narrow down to a few that deal with your subject. If you are unaccustomed to using the Internet, call your state's information hotline. Or look on the reference shelf of the largest local library near you; some states publish booklets describing the grants that are available to their citizens. Your librarian will be able to help you find the volumes you need.

Using the Web

Find everything you need on local, state, and federal grants at **www.firstgov.gov**. For a list of federal grants, go to the Catalog of Federal Domestic Assistance Programs at **www.cfda.gov**, a government-wide list of 1,479 federal programs that provide grants, loans, loan guarantees, services, information, scholarships, training, insurance, and other benefits. From Abandoned Infants to Youth Opportunity Grants, the alphabetical listing of programs is easy to follow.

For other indexes, including one sorted by beneficiaries (like families, youth, or senior citizens), go to **aspe.os.dhhs.gov/cfda**. Also, get tips on developing and writing federal grant proposals at **www.cfda.gov/public/cat-writing.htm**.

city and town grants

A petition may work best

Finding out about government grants from a city or town is a little harder than finding federal grants. That's because a number of cities and towns don't list themselves as funders in the traditional sources. Does that mean that you will have to look elsewhere for funding? Not necessarily. After all, city councils and other representative bodies in smaller towns are often open to grassroots projects developed by their citizens.

Consider petitioning the city council for funding. They sometimes take on philanthropic causes and make them part of the city's budget. If you win them over to your cause, they can work to see that a project gets at least some of its funding directly from the city.

The federal government awards many cities Community Development Block Grants (CDBG). These are often the most accessible funds for grants of $5,000 to $50,000 from your city government.

When considering an appeal to city government for assistance with your project, do not overlook the possibility of asking for in-kind donations of goods and/or services. After all, it might be impossible for a small city budget to stretch enough to help your project. But if you do a bit of research, you might find real estate the city owns that you could ask to be assigned to your project. If rooms in a city-owned building are going unused, getting permission to use them for your project would save you the expense of paying rent. For instance, an after-school reading project might be allowed to hold tutoring sessions in school classrooms. A literacy program or a historical society might find space in the corner of a public library. A municipal hospital might offer an office to a visiting nurse program.

ASK THE EXPERTS

How can I find out if my project is located in a community already targeted for governmental assistance, which would make it more likely to get funded?

Your city mayor's office or the county offices will be able to tell you the locations of local empowerment zones, enterprise communities, or specially designated areas in unincorporated regions. If the people your project will serve are in any of those areas, you have a better chance of getting government grants. You can also check the Web site for the U.S. Department of Housing and Urban Development (**www.hud.gov**).

Will getting a government grant help or hurt me in getting grants from private donors?

Projects that have any kind of support are more likely to get grants from other sources—local city governments and private local donors alike. It doesn't matter if the support is monetary or in-kind donations. Private donors believe that if those who are closest to the project like it enough to help with its support, then it must be worthwhile.

FIRST PERSON DISASTER STORY
Read the Instructions

It was just a matter of one day. I couldn't get the application for my grant to the government agency by its due date of January 4 because my little boy was sick with the flu. The next morning I drove 100 miles into the city and dropped off the application. I explained the whole thing to the receptionist. A couple of months passed, and we called to see if they had made a decision about our request for a grant. We wanted to get started as soon as possible. Imagine how upset I was when I found that our application was not even considered because it had come in a day late. They don't make any exceptions on these application guidelines, even for personal problems. I should have had my husband drop it off the day it was due.

—Laurie L., Dover, Delaware

grading
government grants

It's true that the government has hundreds of millions of dollars to give away, but tracking down the agencies and filling out their forms is not for the faint of heart. If you want to apply for a government grant, pay special attention to the application guidelines. Following instructions in submitting a proposal for any kind of grant is always important, but with a government application, every i must be dotted and every t crossed. Even the smallest variation from their instructions will get the whole proposal tossed before a decision maker ever sees it.

Some agencies offer a workshop in preparing their applications. Take it. If the agency offers no advisory sessions, ask the program officer if there are any special guidelines. (See page 140 for info on calling funders.) You might even want to take a rough draft of your application/proposal to the program officer before it's due and ask for a critique. That way you will know if your entry will be competitive.

Who decides which grants get funded and how? Government grants are graded on a point system. These points are awarded by a committee of peers who review grant proposals.

It's a good idea to ask a program officer at a prospective donor agency how the grading system works. Some agencies offer extra points for extra effort, such as including a local survey showing your project has community support. And some delete points for a sloppy application, such as not including the required number of endorsement letters.

Find Extra Help in Government Publications

Every federal government agency and some state agencies send out a variety of publications that can be helpful to grantseekers. They discuss grants that have been awarded, and just as valuable, they are written in the language you will want to learn in order to be able to write an effective grant proposal. Send a request for publications to the agency in which you are interested, or go to the agency's Web site and search for "publications" or "resources."

The names of these publications can vary—**journals, bulletins, fact sheets**—but they can help you immerse yourself in the big picture of the particular category that your project deals with. The publications are especially good sources of evaluation statistics on current and previous programs that can be used as references in your grant proposal.

For example, the Federal Register, the official daily record of the federal government, has the most comprehensive information on government-funded projects and funding availability. Find it at **www.access.gpo.gov/su_docs/aces/aces140.html**. The home page is below.

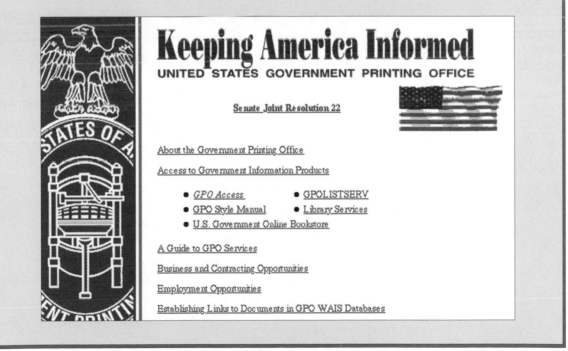

the application

Taking great care in filling it out will be rewarded

Most government grants require that you fill out an application form. The standard form, the SF-424, is the basic form used for most federal government grants. When applying for some grants, you will need to fill out additional forms as well.

Print a copy of SF-424 from **www.cfda.gov/public/sf424.pdf**. Be sure that you print out the accompanying instructions as well as the form you see here. They give detailed guidelines for using the form as part of your application for a federal grant.

One peculiar item explained in the instructions on the back of SF-424 is something called the **State Single Point of Contact** (SPOC). It refers to states that require you to submit federal grant proposals to the state government first for review. A majority of states require this review; 22 do not. (See page 114 for a list of those states.) To submit your proposal for review, you will need to find the name of the agency in your state that governs the SPOC. If you search the Internet for "state single point of contact," you will find the state office you should write to in the **cfda.gov** listings. Or call your state government information line for the address.

Once you find the correct address where you can send your SPOC query, write or e-mail to ask to have instructions sent to you; they will differ from state to state. Many states ask only that you send a brief abstract of the proposal along with the name of the grant you are applying for and the number of its listing in *The Catalog of Federal Domestic Assistance*. Other states may ask for a more complete description of your proposal. Once your proposal has been approved, the state office assigns it a reference number that goes on the federal form (see line item #16 at right).

Tip: All federal application forms have expiration dates. Make sure you are using the current version of the form or your application can be rejected.

APPLICATION FOR
FEDERAL ASSISTANCE

OMB Approval No. 0348-0043

2. DATE SUBMITTED	Applicant Identifier

1. TYPE OF SUBMISSION:		3. DATE RECEIVED BY STATE	State Application Identifier

1. TYPE OF SUBMISSION:

Application
- ☐ Construction
- ☐ Non-Construction

Preapplication
- ☐ Construction
- ☐ Non-Construction

3. DATE RECEIVED BY STATE	State Application Identifier
4. DATE RECEIVED BY FEDERAL AGENCY	Federal Identifier

5. APPLICANT INFORMATION

Legal Name:

Organizational Unit:

Address (give city, county, State, and zip code):

Name and telephone number of person to be contacted on matters involving this application (give area code)

6. EMPLOYER IDENTIFICATION NUMBER (EIN):

☐☐ – ☐☐☐☐☐☐☐

7. TYPE OF APPLICANT: (enter appropriate letter in box) ☐

A. State	H. Independent School Dist.
B. County	I. State Controlled Institution of Higher Learning
C. Municipal	J. Private University
D. Township	K. Indian Tribe
E. Interstate	L. Individual
F. Intermunicipal	M. Profit Organization
G. Special District	N. Other (Specify) _____

8. TYPE OF APPLICATION:

☐ New ☐ Continuation ☐ Revision

If Revision, enter appropriate letter(s) in box(es) ☐ ☐

A. Increase Award B. Decrease Award C. Increase Duration
D. Decrease Duration Other(specify):

_____

9. NAME OF FEDERAL AGENCY:

10. CATALOG OF FEDERAL DOMESTIC ASSISTANCE NUMBER:

☐☐ – ☐☐☐

TITLE:

11. DESCRIPTIVE TITLE OF APPLICANT'S PROJECT:

12. AREAS AFFECTED BY PROJECT (Cities, Counties, States, etc.):

13. PROPOSED PROJECT		14. CONGRESSIONAL DISTRICTS OF:	
Start Date	Ending Date	a. Applicant	b. Project

15. ESTIMATED FUNDING:

a. Federal	$	00
b. Applicant	$	00
c. State	$	00
d. Local	$	00
e. Other	$	00
f. Program Income	$	00
g. TOTAL	$	00

16. IS APPLICATION SUBJECT TO REVIEW BY STATE EXECUTIVE ORDER 12372 PROCESS?

a. YES. THIS PREAPPLICATION/APPLICATION WAS MADE AVAILABLE TO THE STATE EXECUTIVE ORDER 12372 PROCESS FOR REVIEW ON:

DATE _____

b. No. ☐ PROGRAM IS NOT COVERED BY E. O. 12372
☐ OR PROGRAM HAS NOT BEEN SELECTED BY STATE FOR REVIEW

17. IS THE APPLICANT DELINQUENT ON ANY FEDERAL DEBT?

☐ Yes If "Yes," attach an explanation. ☐ No

18. TO THE BEST OF MY KNOWLEDGE AND BELIEF, ALL DATA IN THIS APPLICATION/PREAPPLICATION ARE TRUE AND CORRECT, THE DOCUMENT HAS BEEN DULY AUTHORIZED BY THE GOVERNING BODY OF THE APPLICANT AND THE APPLICANT WILL COMPLY WITH THE ATTACHED ASSURANCES IF THE ASSISTANCE IS AWARDED.

a. Type Name of Authorized Representative	b. Title	c. Telephone Number
d. Signature of Authorized Representative		e. Date Signed

Previous Edition Usable
Authorized for Local Reproduction

Standard Form 424 (Rev. 7-97)
Prescribed by OMB Circular A-102

Source: U.S. Government Printing Office

now what do I do?

I've heard that the chances of being awarded a government grant improve if I show plans to sign up a consultant from outside my organization to evaluate my program's effectiveness. Where can I find such an objective evaluator?

Local colleges and community organizations may be able to help you find people who have obtained government grants in the past. You may also find someone by checking **www.grantprofessionals.org** and **www.wmich.edu/evalctr** on the Internet.

Is there online help for creating a budget for a federal grant?

Go to **www.whitehouse.gov/omb/grants/sf424a.pdf** and you will see a budget that you can print out or save to your computer. It was created for use in applying for federal grants. (It is equally helpful for creating budgets for applications outside of government.)

What are the states that do not require that federal grants be first submitted to them?

The 22 states that do not are: Alabama, Alaska, Colorado, Connecticut, Hawaii, Idaho, Kansas, Louisiana, Massachusetts, Minnesota, Montana, Nebraska, New Jersey, Ohio, Oklahoma, Oregon, Pennsylvania, South Dakota, Tennessee, Vermont, Virginia, and Washington.

What makes a grant proposal stand out from all the others an agency gets?

Agencies like to fund projects that solve a problem, preferably a new and pressing problem. For instance, training senior high school students as tutors in an after-school reading program for disadvantaged first graders. But the bottom line is still the bottom line: Show that your organization can meet the community's need cheaper, faster, and better. This doesn't mean putting down other groups that are doing similar work. In fact, funders like to see community groups working together. For example, name the other groups in your area working on a problem and explain how you'll work together or make joint purchases in bulk to cut costs.

I noticed that government grants ask for my congressional district number, as well as the district numbers for my state assembly and senate. Where do I find these numbers?

Call your local state senator's office, borough hall, or local library. Someone there should be able to provide you with the correct district numbers. Some government agencies use congressional district numbers to track the constituency of the grants they give. And don't forget that district numbers and their boundaries can change with a process called redistricting (or, more cynically, gerrymandering). It always pays to verify that you have the most current information, especially with something as important as a grant proposal. You can also find this information online at **www.congress.org** or by contacting the League of Women Voters at 202-429-1965 (**www.lwv.org**).

Is there one place that lists government agencies and their grants?

Yes, there is a new one-stop portal. Go to **www.firstgov.gov** to find local, state, and federal grant information.

Now Where Do I Go?

BOOKS

Catalog of Federal Domestic Assistance
U.S. Government Printing Office

Grant Writing for Dummies
By Bev Browning

For the People: 1,608 Ways to Get Your Share of the Little-Known Bargains the Government Offers
Edited by Kevin Ireland

21st Century Complete Guide to Federal Grants: The Official Catalog of Federal Domestic Assistance for Loans, Grants, Surplus Equipment and Training
U.S. Government Printing Office

Free Money From the Federal Government, a Series
By Laurie Blum
  Free Money for Small Businesses
    and E ntrepreneurs
  Free Money for Private Schools
  Free Money for Seniors and Their Families
  Free Money for Childhood Behavioral
    and Genetic Disorders
  Free Money for Children's
    Medical/Dental Expenses
  Free Money for Diseases of Aging
  Free Money for Heart Disease and Cancer Care
  Free Money for Infertility Treatments
  Free Money for Mental/Emotional Disorders

Grants for individuals

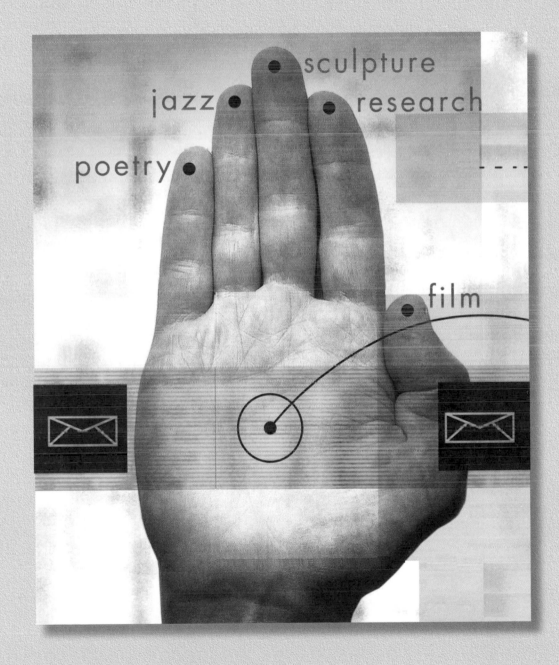

who gets them?

Grants for artists, playwrights, researchers, and other regular folk

Grants are not just for big nonprofit groups. Individuals can receive them, too. If you work as a solo artist, sculptor, writer, photographer, or inventor, you will find a slew of grants created especially for you. The only advantage nonprofit organizations have is that they don't pay taxes on their grant money. Individuals do.

But applying for an individual grant is less gruesome than the full-scale grant process. Typically, you need to describe your project, figure the money you want for it, and include samples of your work and a recommendation or two from a professional in the field. This usually means getting letters of recommendation from a mentor or an endorsement from a recognized expert in your field. Recommendations reassure foundations and other donors that your project has the support of a qualified person or agency. The decision makers at foundations aren't always experts on the subjects in which they award grants, and they welcome evidence of your proposal's worthiness.

Foundations also like to see that your project has ties to the community. For instance, if you are a writer who wants to finish a novel, you might move to the top of a donor's list if you propose to teach writing classes at a community center. If you are a historian, you might find ready support for preserving a local building if you suggest conducting tours for students there.

ASK THE EXPERTS

Where should I start my search for individual grants?

Start with the Foundation Center's resource book *Foundation Grants to Individuals*. This lists 4,300 entries about donors who give grants for individuals. It includes grants for students, artists, company employees, international applicants, and professional researchers.

I am concerned about how much money to ask for. What if I don't spend it all?

Next to finding the right donor, asking for the right amount of money is probably the most important thing. Ask your colleagues for feedback about what you think you need. The budget that you submit with your application should be compiled very carefully. If you ask for too much, you will have to give back what you don't use. If you ask for too little and later have to appeal for additional funds, the donor's coffers may be empty.

Who determines if my work qualifies for a grant?

Most foundations have a group of experts to review the work of individuals seeking the grant. For example, if you are a poet seeking a writing grant, your poetry would be reviewed by a panel of established poets and editors. The makeup of these panels changes from year to year, so if your grant is denied, you might try again and have better luck with a new panel of experts.

if you are a student

**Hitting the books—
with a big wad of
scholarship money**

Grants for students? Yes, there are a lot. They go by many names: scholarships, fellowships, internships. But even though they may come from public and private foundations, the funding often goes directly to the colleges to administer. This means that the application for the scholarship you want often goes through the school's financial aid office instead of directly to a foundation. So before you go trolling through donor lists for a grant, explore the financial aid office at your college or university.

Next, look to local sources for grant money, such as civic and religious organizations. Your church, synagogue, or mosque may give scholarships. Also check with business and social clubs, even if your parents are not members. Many of these organizations like to help sponsor the education of promising young people from their city. Ask at companies where your parents work. Some employers may offer assistance to employees' children for college expenses.

After those sources have been exhausted, look at the possibility of funding from private foundations, including corporate foundations. Some of the larger foundations put aside money each year for student scholarships. But don't leave out the smaller foundations. Many are devoted solely to education. Keep an eye out for restrictions, though. Many donors give only to students within a certain geographic region, those from a specific religion, or those who have other particular interests or characteristics. One Midwestern foundation awards scholarships to left-handed students.

Types of Grants for Students

Scholarships Amounts given to undergraduate—and sometimes graduate—students to cover some or all of their tuition and sometimes books and living expenses.

Fellowships Awards made to graduate students for tuition and expenses. May require teaching duties.

Low-Interest loans These are similar to scholarships and fellowships, but the amount granted must be paid back.

Internships Amounts given to pay living expenses while the student works without pay to gain on-the-job experience.

Helpful Resources

SOURCES

FinAid, The Smart Student Guide to Financial Aid
www.finaid.org
Financial aid information site.

www.petersons.com/resources/finance.html
Answers on financing education.

Click on "Find a College" to get to CollegeQuest, Peterson's database of 850,000 college scholarships, awards, grants, and prizes.
www.petersons.com/ugchannel

FastWeb
www.fastweb.com
A scholarship search engine.

Collegeboard.com
www.collegeboard.com
Click on "Paying for College" to find 2,000 grants from noncollege sources.

BOOKS

Dan Cassidy's Worldwide College Scholarship Directory, 5th Edition
By Dan Cassidy

College Board Scholarship Handbook 2000

The Grants Register 2001, 19th Edition
Edited by Louise Baynes

Financial Aid for Research and Creative Activities Abroad: 2002–2004

See also the list of general resources for individuals on page 135.

if you are a filmmaker

Grants, camera, ACTION!

Most filmmaker grants help fund the production of a film or a video. To get these grants, you will need to send in a videotape of your previous work. What will give you the edge in grantland is not just the brilliance of your filmmaking but specific information about your project and your ability to organize and manage it.

When applying for production funding, you are also likely to be asked to send a shooting script of your project, or at least a treatment. This should be as specific as possible about how the film will be shot and what the subject will be. The donors are interested in what is unique about your idea, and specifics are the best way to show that.

If your first submission falls short, committee members at some foundations will tell you how to improve it. Usually you will be allowed to submit a reworked grant proposal for the next application deadline.

FIRST PERSON DISASTER STORY
By Invitation Only

I was new to grant writing and wasn't quite sure about all the terms. A number of the funders I saw gave out something called an award grant. Sounded good to me. I found the perfect funder for my video and applied. Boy, was I embarrassed when I got back a letter saying that they don't take grant proposals, they only award grants that have been nominated by their own committee. How do you get in touch with this committee? A colleague suggested I join some professional filmmaker organizations to start getting my name out there.

—**Clive N., New York, New York**

Types of Grants for Film and Video Projects

Production Fiscal support for various film and video projects.

Archives Grants for preservation projects.

Technology Support for development of new techniques that could be applied to film or video projects.

Research Money given to search for information to be used either for a specific type of film or video project or for compiling historical records about the cinema.

Fellowships Grants for teaching film and video and obtaining advanced degrees.

Helpful Resources

SOURCES

Association of Independent Video and Filmmakers
www.aivf.org

Independent Television Service
www.itvs.org

www.warshawski.com
Provides bibliography on fund-raising for film and video projects.

National Endowment for the Humanities
www.neh.fed.us
Funds documentaries.

New York Foundation for the Arts
www.artswire.org
Supports production of independent films and offers information on fellowships and sponsorship.

National Endowment for the Arts
www.nea.gov

BOOKS

The National Guide to Funding in Arts and Culture, 7th Edition

Grants for Film, Media, and Communications, 2001–2002

Directory of Grants in the Humanities: 2000-2001

The Independent Film and Videomaker's Guide, 2nd Edition
By Michael Wiese

Film and Video Financing
By Michael Wiese

See also the list of general resources for individuals on page 135.

if you are a painter or sculptor

Your work is your passport

Whatever you do, don't send any original artwork with your grant proposal. Foundations can't keep track of it, and the chances of it getting lost are high. Instead, have good photographs and slides made of your best pieces way ahead of your deadline. Your investment will be worth it. If the pictures are good enough, your art will speak for itself—from a safe distance.

Recommendations from leaders in the arts in your community mean a lot to donors and can help your chances of getting a grant. Participate in local art exhibitions and workshops before trying for a grant. This will give you time to build up relationships with people who might be able to write letters on your behalf.

If your proposed project happens to relate to a community activity, all the better. For instance, one art project that got funding used old fabrics donated by a number of elderly people to make art structures. The artist took notes about how the fabric had figured in their lives and displayed the notes next to the artwork.

When you submit a proposal for a project to instruct or mentor a budding artist, show your experience. If you do not have experience, perhaps you can gain some as a temporary intern at a local community center. If not, you might have someone write a recommendation explaining how clearly you are able to talk about art.

Types of Grants for Artists and Sculptors

Fellowships Grants made to allow the individual to work on particular projects, sometimes within a graduate program. May include teaching duties.

Residencies Awards of workspace, usually room and board and sometimes materials and equipment. They often involve interaction with the community, such as lectures, workshops, and programs for children and young people.

General welfare and special needs Amounts given to pay living expenses and medical bills, often on a short-term emergency basis but sometimes for longer periods.

Helpful Resources

SOURCES

Americans for the Arts
www.artsusa.org
Information on funding for all areas of the arts.

www.xensei.com/users/adl
Art deadlines list published monthly.

National Endowment for the Arts
www.arts.endow.gov
Offers information on fellowships for artists.

The Zuzu Petals Literary Resource
www.zuzu.com
Links to grant resources and arts councils.

BOOKS

American Art Directory 2001–2002
Listing of art scholarships and fellowships.

Organization Artists: A Document and Directory of the National Association of Artists' Organizations, 4th Edition

Breaking through the Clutter: Business Solutions for Women, Artists, and Entrepreneurs
By Judith Luther Wilder

Artists Communities: A Directory of Residencies in the United States Offering Time and Space for Creativity, 2nd Edition
Edited by Tricia Snell

See also the list of general resources for individuals on page 135.

if you are a writer

Chapter and verse

Writers need to submit samples of their work, but unlike other artists, they can submit unfinished works—say the first 50 pages of a novel in progress. You may be asked to make multiple copies to go with your application because a committee of writers will be reading your submission and judging your work.

Some applications ask that you submit a resumé and answer essay questions in order to put your work in context. Read the foundation's mission statement and craft your application to point up the parallels in your work and the prospective donor's goals.

As with other art grants, it sometimes pays to research the identities of the committee members who will be judging the submissions, because you can then slant your proposal to their interests. Another good tip: Find out which writers were awarded grants in the past. If your work is in a similar vein they may favor your writing.

If your proposal is rejected, it pays to check back with the donor the next year. The list of judges may have changed. If the new judges favor a style of writing that is similar to yours, your work may be more likely to be received well.

Helpful Resources for Writers

SOURCES

Americans for the Arts
www.artsusa.org
Information on funding for all
areas of the arts.

National Endowment for the Arts
www.arts.endow.gov
Offers information on writing
fellowships.

Poets and Writers Online
www.pw.org/mag/grantsawards.htm
Lists writing prizes.

Zuzu's Petals Literary Resource
www.zuzu.com
Offers links to grant organizations and art
councils.

Newswise
www.newswise.com
Listing of journalism grants.

BOOKS

**Artists Communities: A Directory
of Residencies in the United States
Offering Time and Space for
Creativity, 2nd Edition**
Edited by Tricia Snell

Alliance of Artists' Communities,
Allworth Press, 2000

**Artists and Writers Colonies:
Retreats, Residencies and Respites
for the Creative Mind 2000**
By Robyn Middleton, Mindy Seale,
Martha Ruddley, and Stacey Loomis

**Money for Writers: Over 800 Cash
Awards, Grants, Prizes, Contests,
Scholarships, Retreats, and More**
Edited by Diane Billot

**Grants and Awards Available to
American Writers, 22nd Edition**
Edited by John Morrone

**The Journalist's Road to Success:
A Career and Scholarship Guide**

**Dramatists Sourcebook: Complete
Opportunities for Playwrights,
Translators, Composers, Lyricists,
and Librettists, 2002-03 Edition**
By Gretchen Von Lerte and
Todd Miller

**The Student's Guide to Playwriting
Opportunities, 2nd Edition**
By Michael Wright and Elena Carillo

See also the list of general resources for
individuals on page 135.

if you are a musician

Play and get a grant to do it!

There are grants for all types of music: jazz, bluegrass, pop, classical, marches, ragtime, reggae, and religious, and plenty more. Some donors even narrow it down to a particular time period, such as the earliest plainsong or the most recent rock opera. You can look for grants based on country of origin, ranging from Balinese temple songs to Peruvian highland lullabies. There are also grants for music teachers, for example, to pay the fees to train a gifted but underprivileged student.

Once you have done some of your donor research, ask your contacts in the field for help. Your teachers, coaches, and associates can often steer you to viable funding sources that are suitable for your needs. The network of contacts you may make when you attend conferences and workshops can be especially helpful. You may also benefit from examining the careers of successful musicians in your genre who are slightly older than you. The grants they won and the workshops they attended may indicate a path for you.

If you are a performer, you will have to send in a sample tape of your work with most applications. If that is the case, get the best recording you can afford. Although professional recording can be expensive, it's worth it to get a high-quality tape to make every note clear and give you the best possible chance of winning a grant.

Types of Grants for Musicians

Fellowships Grants made to allow the individual to work on particular composition projects or to attend graduate school. May include teaching duties.

Residencies Awards of studio space, usually with room and board, and possibly mentoring by a well-known musician. They often involve interaction of the artist with the community—for example, lectures, workshops, and programs for children.

Commissions Given for composing projects and sometimes for archival programs.

Recording and touring support Funds for both uses, usually for educational purposes. May also be awarded for development of new recording technology.

General welfare and special needs Amounts given to pay living expenses and/or medical bills, usually on an emergency basis, but sometimes for extended periods.

Archival projects Grants are available to help preserve music from the past, either on paper or in recordings.

Helpful Resources

SOURCES

National Endowment for the Arts
www.arts.cndow.gov
Offers information on music fellowships.

www.sai-national.org
Grant resources for all kinds of music compiled by Sigma Alpha Iota, the international music fraternity.

www.ascap.com/lp_about_ascap.html
Lists prizes and grants to composers.

National Academy of Recording Arts & Sciences
grammy.com
Lists grants for archiving and preserving music and sound heritage.

BMI Foundation
www.bmi.com/bmifoundation/index.asp
Offers programs and support for composers in classical music, jazz, and musical theater.

www.musicalonline.com/foundation_grants.htm
Musical Online listing of grant resources for musicians.

See also the list of general resources for individuals on page 135.

if you want to do research

Foundations, corporations, universities, and hospitals

Research grants are given for just about anything, from analyzing Mexican pottery to finding a cure for cancer. Private foundations offer grants for specialized research, as does the public workhorse of research grants, the National Endowment for the Humanities.

Some corporate foundations are keen to fund research. Their grants are designed to help talented researchers, engineers, or inventors with the resources they need to explore a new theory that could lead to a marketing coup. If you can't find a corporate donor, you may need to make a connection with a university or hospital.

A word of caution: A grant may bind you to a contract or even employment with a particular corporation or school. Check your rights with a lawyer before accepting the grant. Otherwise you may forfeit any future profits from products developed during your research.

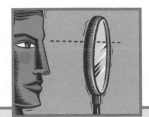

Types of Research Grants

Fellowships Funds for graduate students or on-campus researchers. May include teaching duties.

Project support Grants for professionals to plan and carry out research ventures.

Research Grants given for professional or academic investigative projects, especially in medicine.

Residencies Amounts given to professionals or academics as living expenses to allow study or research in a particular area or near special facilities.

Professional studies Funds given to established professionals to pay for advanced training.

Helpful Resources

SOURCES

Catalog of Federal Domestic Assistance
www.cfda.gov
Lists federal sources for loans, research grants, donations, and technical assistance.

National Endowment for the
Humanities Funds
www.neh.fed.us
Research and education in all areas.

National Institutes of Health
grants.nih.gov/grants/oer.htm
Gives grants for fellowships and research in biomedicine.

National Science Foundation
www.nsf.gov
Offers grants, contracts, and cooperative agreements for research and education in science and engineering.

Social Science Research Council
www.ssrc.org
Gives grants and fellowships.

BOOKS

**The Grants Register 2002,
20th Edition**

**Directory of Biomedical and Health
Care Grants**

Directory of Research Grants

**Financial Aid for Research and
Creative Activities Abroad
1999–2001**
By Gail Ann Schlachter
and David R. Weber

See also the list of general resources for individuals on page 135.

when it pays to affiliate

Benefit by association with a nonprofit

Since most grants are given to nonprofit organizations, you can increase your prospective grant pool by affiliating with a nonprofit group. Your affiliation can be as simple as offering to teach a course at a university in exchange for the university's sponsorship of your grant proposal. Or, it can be as complex as going on staff at a scientific research foundation to get funding for your latest experiment.

Why do donors prefer working through nonprofits? Several reasons.

■ It is cheaper in administrative costs and more efficient for a foundation to give a large amount of money to one institution and have them divide it up than to give grants of small amounts to lots of individuals.

■ To prevent fraud, the IRS imposes stringent rules on a foundation when it offers grants to individuals. If, instead, the foundation gives the money to a nonprofit organization, which in turn gives it to an individual, the foundation is free from that extra layer of IRS regulations.

■ A foundation is not likely to give you funds for equipment, administration, overhead, and facilities, but an institution, such as a college or hospital, is more likely to obtain funding that allows you to use their facilities.

If you decide you'd like to affiliate with a nonprofit group, see chapter 2 for information on how to go about it.

ASK THE EXPERTS

I don't know anyone who runs a nonprofit group. How do I get to know such people so I can affiliate with their group?

You are probably already associated with one or more nonprofit groups and don't even know it. Look at schools, religious groups, libraries, alumni associations, civic groups, trade associations, YMCA, YWCA, and hospitals. If your local nonprofits don't fit the bill, do a little research and make a list of those nonprofits whose mission statements match your goals. Then contact their program directors and pitch them your idea. You will be surprised how warmly most of them will welcome your request. Your project is likely to reflect well on them, bringing them prestige and more connections with prospective donors.

If I get involved with an organization, won't they take over my project?

It is always a possibility, but there are many ways to arrange your connection with the organization. You can use them only as a fiscal agent, or you can take on closer ties. If you word your letter of agreement carefully, you can minimize interference problems. Besides, some interaction may be helpful. If you build a strong association with your sponsoring organization, you may find that your project can be enhanced by their services and facilities—and even the fresh ideas they may bring to the project.

My rich uncle wants to give me money for my research project instead of having me go through the bother of applying for a grant. Can he get a tax write-off for the money he gives me?

The IRS lets anyone give anyone up to $11,000 a year as a gift. But the donor, in this case your uncle, does not get a tax deduction for giving to an individual. The good news is you would not have to pay income taxes on the gift. Because tax laws and interpretations change, consult a tax attorney.

now what do I do?

Answers to common questions

I see that there are several CD's and online services that list foundations that give to individuals. They are much easier to use than those big, bulky books. Can I just stick to the electronic sources when doing my research and forget about the lists in print?

Use both. Wading through the big, bulky books is important for individuals seeking grants. Usually it is the books rather than the electronic lists that include the smaller foundations with limited assets. Those are the most likely to give the smaller grants that go to individuals.

My grant was rejected. Is it okay to reapply for the same grant again for the next deadline?

It depends on why it was rejected. It would be helpful to get some feedback after you are turned down about why it happened. Sometimes foundation staff can be very obliging in steering your next application or even suggesting other potential donors who may be a better fit. If the problem has to do with the judges, you may be better off waiting for a change in the judging committee.

Do I have to pay income taxes on a grant that I get as an individual?

Yes, you do. It is considered income and taxed accordingly.

What is a nomination grant?

In this type of grant, the money is typically given as an award or prize. You cannot apply for these grants; you have to be nominated for them—usually by prominent people in your field.

I sent a videotape of my last play when I submitted my grant. The tape was never returned to me, even when they sent back a letter saying I didn't get the grant. What can I do?

You can ask for its return, but be prepared to learn that the foundation has no way to log in and keep track of all the application materials it receives. Next time you apply, offer a tape in your application, but do not send it unless specifically requested, and then send only an extra copy. A copy of your reviews could be helpful, unless the rules restrict you from sending extra material.

Is it okay for me to keep in touch with the panel of judges who gave me the grant?

It depends. Although it is almost always a very good idea to keep in touch with funders throughout the year, sometimes the judges prefer an arm's-length relationship. Send each one an individual note of thanks (unless forbidden in the guidelines) and invite them to your next show or recital.

There's one foundation that sounds perfect for my needs, but they only give out $1,000 grants, and I need more money. Couldn't they make an exception just once?

It is unlikely. In fact, if you have never received a grant from them before, you probably will do better by asking for less than the maximum. For the rest of the money you need, apply to other foundations, and say you are doing so on your applications. That will show that you are aware of the size limits on the grants, but you are working hard to get funding that is adequate for your project.

Now Where Do I Go?

CONTACTS

The Foundation Center's Online Librarian
www.fndncenter.org
Look for the Learning Lab's Online Librarian.

Council on Foundations
www.cof.org

CD-ROM
FC SEARCH: The Foundation Center's Database on CD-ROM 4.0

BOOKS

Taft directories

The Foundation Directories

The Foundation Center's Guide to Grantseeking on the Web

The Foundation Center's User-Friendly Guide: A Grantseeker's Guide to Resources, 4th Edition

Dramatists Sourcebook: Complete Opportunities for Playwrights, Translators, Composers, Lyricists and Librettists
By Gretchen Von Lerte and Todd Miller

Customizing your work

targeting your funders

Start narrowing the list

You have written a generic boilerplate proposal and hammered out a budget. Moreover, the key people involved with the project have read your proposal and agreed with your words and numbers. Great; good for you! Now what? Remember that list of potential donors you culled from searching through the library and the Internet? And remember, too, those annual reports and 990-PF's that you wrote away for and are now stacked up waiting to be read? Now is the time to go through them. While you read, ask yourself these questions.

Is there a good fit? Check to see that the goal of your project or the work of your sponsoring nonprofit organization fits with the funders' mission. You can find the mission statement in most funder's annual reports.

Do any restrictions apply? Many funders restrict their grants to specific populations, locations, types of grants, and amounts of grants given. Make sure there is nothing in your proposal that would raise a red flag.

Your goal is to winnow down your list to a handful of really good potential donors.

Set up a filing system

Make a file for each funder you are considering approaching. In it, store the funder's annual report, 990-PF's, and any other research. Keep a list by name (in alphabetical order); deadlines, if any; key funding words (such as aged, children, or seed money); and typical awards by size. Use these categories:

$100,000+

$50,000–$100,000

$25,000–$ 50,000

$10,000–$ 25,000

and less than $ 10,000

138

Grant-Giving Patterns

You are looking for a good match between the donor and your proposal. Can you see clear parallels between your project and any other projects that have received grants from this donor during the past few years?

Type of organization Do most of the donor's funds go to large, well-established organizations? To individuals? To small, community-based groups? Even if your project fits the donor's aims, it may not appeal to the donor because of its size, geographic location, or other characteristics.

Amount of money requested Are you asking for a great deal more than this donor typically awards to a single project? Or less? Adjust the amount to fit the donor's past pattern, or choose another donor.

Number of grants per year Are they many and varied? If so, you may have a better chance than if there are only a few. Some foundations exist only as go-betweens for tax-free gifts from an individual to one or two specific organizations and may not be interested in other possibilities.

How Much Do They Give?

Look carefully at the size of the grants a prospective donor has been giving during the past few years. If you are applying for the first time, you are not likely to get the top amount. It's better to start by asking for a figure comparable to their smallest awards, or no more than the average, and either cut the size of your program or get the rest of your funding from other sources. Once you have a working relationship with the donor, you can ask for bigger grants.

calling the donor

Think like a business partner

Found some good possibilities? Great. Now get ready to begin the dialogue with your funder-to-be. You are no longer just an inquiring researcher, you are a potential partner. Call the funder's office and ask to speak to the **program officer**—the person in charge of administrating the grant you are interested in getting.

Why call? The first reason is to make sure the information you have about the funder is the most up-to-date. When you call, start by introducing yourself and give the name of your agency, its location, and its basic goals. Then state why you are calling: You want to know if there have been any updates about the

donor since the annual reports or other materials you have were published. You are not calling to make a pitch for your project. You are calling simply to gather firsthand information.

If no major changes have been made, and the program officer has the time, inquire if the funder is venturing into any new directions regarding its funding. Sometimes funders embrace new trends in funding that might help or hinder your getting a grant. For example, since the 9/11 attacks, a number of funders have given grants related to homeland security and that information may or may not have made it into their annual reports or Web sites.

Next, ask for the latest instructions on applying for a grant. Some donors request that you fill out an **application form**, which they will send you, while others may prefer that you write a **letter of intent** or inquiry briefly explaining your project. If they like the letter they will ask you to submit a grant proposal. Still others want you to go ahead and submit a proposal with just a cover letter. The point is to comply with the way each donor likes to be approached.

ASK THE EXPERTS

I couldn't get through to the program officer, but the receptionist was able to answer most of my questions. Is that okay?

Yes. What you want is the most recent information, specifically in regard to deadlines for mailing out your proposal. And you want information about how to apply. Be courteous to whoever gives you that information. Once you get the application instructions, you may have a question that only the program officer can answer. If that is the case, write it out and e-mail it (if that is acceptable) or mail it. Program officers are often swamped with phone calls asking for basic information that appears on the funder's Web site or annual report.

Call Report

When you call a funder, take notes. On a piece of paper, write down the date and time of the call, the phone number, the name and title of the person you spoke with, and the subjects you discussed. File this paper in that funder's file. This is known as a call report, and you can develop a form for this information (see below). It will help you keep track of whom you've talked to, when, and what your conversation covered.

CALL REPORT

Name of Organization

Date

Name of Contact

Title

Subject Discussed

Summary of Conversation

Notes (your own reaction to what was said)

customizing your words

Use the donor's words, phrases, and terms

Use the information you gathered about the donor to your advantage when you fill out your application, write your letter of intent, or most important of all—when you personalize your proposal so the donor feels it is just their cup of tea.

The more you read about a foundation, the more you can make their phrases your own. Go over the description of the foundation's purpose and activities in its annual report. Then see if you can modify the wording of your proposal to use any of their language. This may sound like blatant pandering, but it is not. You are showing that you agree with their aims. When large amounts of money are at stake, a foundation or other donor appreciates knowing that your purpose is identical to their own.

When you have finished, you will have a new version of your proposal that is ready to send to this specific donor. It will emphasize the aspects of your project that reflect this donor's interests. If you have succeeded in customizing your generic, boilerplate proposal, this version is uniquely suited to one prospective donor. Don't use it for any other donor; keep it in a separate file.

The Foundation is dedicated to the enhancement of the quality of life. Its interest is focused on public educational institutions with programs that encourage higher levels of achievement, further basic skills and enrichment, promote professional development, enhance curricula, increase parental involvement and encourage the pursuit of higher education among the less affluent. The Foundation also supports the efforts of private institutions to provide educational opportunities for the economically disadvantaged.

The Foundation considers requests from health and human services organizations to support programs designed to help the underserved, disadvantaged and at-risk populations achieve fuller and more meaningful participation in the community, and to address issues of hunger and homelessness.

Support is also given to community development-related activities designed to expand the Baltimore region's economic base, job opportunities, tourism and neighborhood revitalization. Workforce development initiatives designed to meet the needs of the unemployed and underemployed are of interest.

The Foundation provides funds to selected cultural organizations that are committed to building a diverse base of support and conducting strong outreach and educational programs. It also supports programs that seek to preserve Maryland's ecologically significant and endangered natural resources.

Only organizations with 501(c)(3) tax-exempt status are funded. Three types of grants are awarded: planning, seed funding (for start-up and demonstration projects) and capital. Though grants are awarded on a one-time basis, the Foundation may make multi-year grants in exceptional cases. Decisions on the Foundation's funding preferences rest on criteria which include:

1. Demonstration of need;
2. Clearly defined goals and objectives;
3. Evidence of strong fiscal management and ongoing

Make the language in your proposal similar to the language used by the donor.

the application

Filling out the form

Many prospective donors have their own application forms that they want you to complete instead of sending a narrative proposal. Government funders always insist upon an application form. In some cases, you can find a funder's application form on the Web site. You can download it from the Internet onto your computer, and if you have the appropriate software, you can fill it out and even e-mail it back. (If you don't have the same software as the funder, you will have to download the form, print it out, fill it in manually, and mail it back.) In other cases, you have to ask for the application over the phone and wait to receive it in the mail. Follow the guidelines.

An application is nothing more than a list of questions about your organization and your project. Use phrases from your boilerplate proposal to answer the questions. (See a sample grant-winning proposal based on an application on page 184.)

You will probably come across a question asking if you have applied elsewhere for support. If you have, answer truthfully. It won't necessarily work against you. Besides, those in the non-profit world know each other's programs and may be acquainted personally as well as professionally. If you apply elsewhere, your prospective donor is likely to hear about your efforts.

TIP: If you have never filled out a grant application, it's a good idea to make a photocopy of the form and fill that out in pencil. It's a lot easier to make changes that way. When you have a perfect version, fill out the real form in ink or on your computer.

▸GRANTSEEKING

Online Grant Application – Online Form

Step 2 - Tell Us About Your Proposal

Please enter your proposal information in our online form. You may find it easier to compose your information in a word processor and then paste the finished text into our form.

Red **fields are required**

Purpose Statement: (40-50 word limit)
A purpose statement is a concise overview of what the funding request is for, including targeted audience(s).

Total Dollar Amount Requested:

Total Budget of the project if different:

Project Objectives and Proposed Activities:

Time Schedules or Anticipated Duration of Proposed Grant:

Anticipated Outcomes:

Personnel and Financial Resources Available:

Sustainability Strategy:
The grantee, community, or other beneficiary must demonstrate the potential to continue the funded work in a self-renewing manner after Kellogg Foundation funding ceases.

Submit

Some funders, like the W.K. Kellogg Foundation, let you fill out an application online.

a letter of intent

It's a short, sweet version of your proposal

Some funders skip the application process and ask for a **letter of intent**—a little summary of what your project is all about. If the program officer likes your letter, she will contact you and ask you to send the full proposal.

What exactly is in this letter of intent, also called a **letter of inquiry?** It contains the same sections as your proposal, but streamlined so that each section is two concise sentences. How long is a letter of intent? Usually no more than three pages. Less complex projects may need only one page. Do not include attachments unless the guidelines suggest it.

As you write the letter, remember to keep the funder's mission and language in mind. Explaining how your project fulfills the

prospect's funding guidelines is key. When you have finished writing a draft of the letter, leave it alone for an hour or so (or overnight, if possible), then read it again. At this second reading, you may find you want to edit the letter to make it clearer or more concise. Keep in mind that you don't have to describe every detail here. Just give an inviting picture of the project. The executive director of your nonprofit sponsor should sign the letter. (See page 182 for a sample of a letter of intent.)

ASK THE EXPERTS

I've sent the letter of intent. Now what do I do?

You can either wait for the funder to contact you or take the bull by the horns and call them. Ask to speak to the person to whom you addressed the letter of intent, probably the donor's executive director or a program officer. This call can be nerve-racking, so be calm and have a copy of your letter and your boiler-plate proposal on hand. Ask first if the letter was received. If it was, ask if your project is something the organization is interested in funding. If yes, then ask about the next steps. Typically, a funder will want to see a full-blown proposal. Or he may ask to meet with your organization to review your project firsthand. Either way, you made the cut. Congratulations. If the answer is no, be considerate and thank him for his time, but ask if you can get some feedback as to why your proposal was rejected.

I called, and the funder wants to meet with us. What should we do?

Celebrate! You are on your way. Once you are finished celebrating, get down to work and prepare for a topflight meeting. You want to have all the key people there (for example, the executive director, board chair or president, and program director) to present the vital aspects of your project. Ideally, you should have an agenda for the meeting and send it to the donor's program officer a few days beforehand. Be sure to include directions to the meeting place. (For more information on arranging a meeting, see page 164.)

customizing your proposal

Keep the funder's guidelines in mind

Okay, it's now time to send out a proposal. Do you just slap the donor's name on the cover letter, make the required copies, and send it off? That's not the smartest way to go. Take a little more time and customize your proposal to the funder's needs and proposal guidelines.

First, review their proposal guidelines for any unusual items. The guidelines are like a kit with instructions to help put your proposal together. (In fact, they are often called **grant kits**.) For example, some funders provide checklists for you to mark as you complete each required task.

Next, note any specific restrictions. For instance, funders may not fund administrative costs. If you have administrative costs in your budget, you may want to put them in the "other expenses" category and break out the bigger items like telephones and utilities. The more easily expenses can be considered direct costs of the project, the more likely they are to be accepted. Government donors typically have specific restrictions about the evaluation section of a proposal and require certain methods be used at set intervals.

Second, review the funder's preparation guidelines. Be prepared for some tedious rules and regulations. Some funders specify everything from type size to margin widths. Some want 2 copies, some want 12. Some want lots of supporting documents, some want none. (See page 156.)

Remember as you revise your proposal to keep the funder's mission and language in mind. You want your proposal to fit into the donor's organization—you want to form a partnership. Make your language inviting and compelling. (See page 142.)

TIP: Always follow the funder's rules or guidelines. If there aren't any, use good taste and clear judgment.

Checklist for a Winning Proposal

❑ Cover letter

❑ Focused, clear statement of need

❑ Course of action

❑ Timeline

❑ Plan and sources for future funding

❑ List of Board of Directors and key
   staff and skills they bring to
   the program/project

❑ IRS 501(c) 3 letter

❑ Graphs, drawings, charts

❑ Brief history of organization and mission statement

❑ Objective(s)

❑ Collaborative partner organizations

❑ Evaluation of criteria

❑ Budget

❑ List other organizations who have given support
   to this program/project

❑ Latest audit

❑ Signatures of all the required people

General Proposal Tips

❑ Focus on those you serve

❑ Follow the guidelines

❑ Build relationships with and
   listen to the foundation staff

❑ Confirm foundation receipt
   of proposal

❑ Ask for feedback from foundation

❑ Quantify whenever you can

❑ Break the writing down into small sections

❑ Proofread

❑ Follow up with developing news

❑ Thank the foundation

multiple proposals

When you are applying to more than one foundation or agency or corporation (the more the better), it is important to keep information about each prospective donor separate. In the course of raising funds, running a project, and juggling evaluations, it's easy to get the particulars about your possible benefactors confused. If you keep the files for donors separate, it will help greatly when you are customizing your proposal.

If your project is complex and expensive, you may want to consider searching for multiple donors. How do you do that? Break up your budget into several different chunks and ask different funders to take on only one piece of the project. Perhaps one chunk could be for the consultants. Another could be for the personnel. Still another might be for transportation or for the space needed.

Match the size of your requests to grants the funders have given in the past. Your goal is to minimize your monetary request, because it is more likely to be accepted if it is not very large. Then, once you're in, you can ask for more.

If you happen to get funding from several donors in excess of your needs, you don't necessarily have to give the money back. Instead, propose ways to expand your project. Can it serve twice as many people? Can it include more related activities? Can it continue for an extra year? Write some very grateful letters to your benefactors, then propose the expansion.

FIRST PERSON DISASTER STORY
Oops! I Forgot to Change the Name!

I knew enough not to do a mass mailing of our grant proposal. Everyone said that was a surefire way to get rejected. And so I studied each of the six funders I knew would be good candidates and worked on tweaking my language so each one got a customized version of our proposal. It took a lot of work, but I did it. A few weeks after I mailed out the proposals, I called to check that they had arrived. That's when I learned that I had forgotten to change the name of the foundation the few times I mentioned it within the proposal. All six foundations got customized versions, but all mentioned the first funder in the proposal. What a huge mistake. Two rejected us outright for this error, but the other four were nice about it and let me resubmit new proposals with the correct foundation name in place.

—Erika M., San Francisco, California

now what do I do?

Answers to common questions

I am trying to fill out application forms from a foundation and a couple of government agencies, and they don't have enough room for my answers. Can I attach a separate sheet?

No, because the space provided indicates the length of answer that is preferred. It is better to write a more concise version of your answer than to give an answer that is too long. You might check with the program officer if you feel you have a special case that genuinely needs more space, but generally it isn't a good idea.

A friend wrote a cover letter for our proposal that thanked the foundation for considering our request. It sounded so cloying. Is this necessary?

Absolutely. You will not be able to thank a donor or prospective donor enough. If you have any feeling of restraint when it comes to expressing your thanks at every step, it might be wise to find someone else to handle all the correspondence and contact with donors for your project. Some of the most successful letters have even thanked a foundation for its very interest in chosen fields of endeavor and their past history of support for projects run by other organizations. People who give to nonprofit causes are invariably gratified when their efforts and largesse are recognized.

How likely is it that I will get a grant for my project?

Your chances are good if you have a good idea; have community support; identify prospective donors who are interested in projects such as yours; send in clearly written, well-researched proposals; and follow the rules set up for the grant that you want. Be patient. If you don't get a grant during the first round of proposals you send out, you can review your work and ask the donor what went wrong. Most people who work in philanthropy are caring, helpful people by nature who will be glad to advise you. Maybe your proposal is better suited for another organization. Some foundation staffers may even recommend another donor who would be perfect for you! You may also revise your proposal and send it to the original donor the following year. Many people try several times before they finally land a grant.

One foundation to which I mailed an application and a proposal said on their guidelines "no personal phone calls." Should I call anyway?

No. Instead, follow up by sending a letter, but even then you may not get a reply. Some foundations aren't staffed to handle personal contacts.

Recently I called a funder to ask about applying for a grant. I got tongue-tied when the program officer asked me questions about the project. What should I have done?

When you call a program officer, be prepared to describe your project briefly on the phone if you are asked. To do this, have your proposal introduction or executive summary in front of you so you can be articulate. Underlining key phrases in yellow and rehearsing will help you enunciate them.

Now Where Do I Go?

CONTACTS

The Foundation Center's Associates Program
www.fdncenter.org/marketplace

The Foundation Directory Online
www.fdncenter.org/marketplace
Both are subscription services.

CD-ROMS

FCSearch: The Foundation Center's Database
Compiled by the Foundation Center annually.

BOOKS

Guide to U.S. Foundations, Their Trustees, Officers, and Donors
Compiled by the Foundation Center annually.

The Foundation 1000
Compiled by the Foundation Center annually.

The Foundation Grants Index
Compiled by the Foundation Center annually.

National Directory of Corporate Giving
Compiled by the Foundation Center annually.

Directory of New and Emerging Foundations
Compiled by the Foundation Center annually.

Foundation Giving: Yearbook on Facts and Figures on Private, Corporate, and Community Foundations
Compiled by the Foundation Center annually.

Public Media Center's Index of Progressive Funders

Source Book Profiles
Compiled by the Foundation Center annually.

CHAPTER 9

Sending off your proposal

preparing the document

Follow the rules to the letter

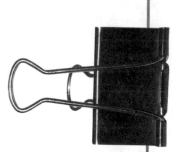

Now it's down to the nitty gritty. Resist the urge to prepare your proposal as you would a regular letter or document. You need to follow the funder's preparation guidelines. Here's what most funders typically request.

Paper Plain white 8 1/2-by-11-inch paper is best. Most donors object to your using fancy paper because they think it's a waste of money and unnecessary.

Extra copies Send only one copy, unless the application instructions request more. If they do want more copies, remember to factor the copying time into your mailing schedule.

Type Unless the application instructions say otherwise, the document should be printed in 12-point type and Times Roman or Times New Roman typeface. The standard look is what they want. Conformity works.

> 10 point Times Roman
>
> ✔ 12 point Times Roman
>
> 14 point Times Roman

My Grant Proposal

No binding or staples The program officer or staff will take the proposal apart as soon as it comes into the office to copy and distribute according to their internal procedure. Use a binder clip or put a rubber band around the papers.

Margins and spacing Unless otherwise instructed, use 1-inch margins all around. Single-space text with double spacing between paragraphs.

Page numbers They help, but make them inconspicuous. (Don't put any on the cover letter or first page of the proposal.) It's a good idea to have your proposal's initials in small type near the page number in case pages get separated; for example, Education for Educators Collaboration would use EEC-7.

TIP: A proposal that is hard to read is one of the top complaints of foundation staffers. Make yours easy to read. Remember, donors are reading hundreds of these things!

the cover letter

Make it vital and compelling

It's almost over, honest. You just need to write one more thing: the **cover letter.** This is a succinct description of your project and why it needs support. Because the cover letter is the first thing a busy program officer will see of your proposal, it needs to be brief (no more than one page or a page-and-a-half), but very, very compelling. To many program directors, the cover letter is the make-or-break document; it either intrigues them enough to keep reading or leaves them cold enough to reject your proposal outright.

What should you write in a cover letter? Start off by explaining why you are approaching this particular funder for a specific amount of grant money. Mention the work of the funder in the past and how it matches your project perfectly. If you have talked

with the program director, mention the conversation.

The next few paragraphs should explain your project and your organization. Your language needs to be expressive and vital. Use adjectives and metaphors to make the text human and interesting. Your job is to show that your project is filling a critical need; use real-life examples to make your point. Also, describe any past successes your organization has had and what it hopes to accomplish in the future.

End the letter with a brief list of the documents enclosed, such as the proposal, financial statements, letters of endorsement, and so on. This letter needs to be signed by the executive director of your organization.

Sample Cover Letter

Growing Great Readers Project
Thursdon Hills Elementary School
P. O. Box 2722
Thursdon Hills, GA 00000

November 13, 2003

Robert Grantmaker
Executive Director
XYZ Corporation
Founders Way, New York 00000

Dear Mr. Grantmaker:

Include grant amount and note funder's interest in issues

Because of your interest in and support for primary education projects in Georgia, we ask that you give consideration to funding our project for $45,000. Our concern at Thursdon Hills Elementary School is that our children cannot read as well as other children in the state. According to the state's most recent report, 57% of our children read below grade level at the end of their first school year. In order to improve our children's reading proficiency, our Parent Teachers Association (PTA) is instituting after-school workshops in the Growing Great Readers Project.

Describe your organization

The Growing Great Readers Project is just the latest of a score of initiatives developed by the PTA at Thursdon Hills Elementary School. During the years since its inception, the PTA has established a fund-raising tradition for special projects at the school that upgrade teacher skills, provide special field trips, obtain special equipment for the classrooms, and train parents how to help their children learn.

Describe project

Our Growing Great Readers Project will be directed by a professional reading specialist who will train volunteer retirees from nearby retirement communities as tutors. Not only will all of our children receive expert help with their reading, but their parents will also be trained to assist them with reading homework and special assignments.

The retirees who will be tutors are not the only people in our community who will be involved. As you will see in our proposal, we have support from several local merchants for in-kind and financial aid.

List what is enclosed

We appreciate your consideration of our proposal. Enclosed please find the proposal, budget, and letters of endorsement. If you have any questions or need additional information, please do not hesitate to contact me at 000-000-0000.

Sincerely yours,

V. L. Onima
Executive Director

assembling the package

Cover letter, cover
page, budget,
501(c)3 form,
table of contents,
and articles

Okay, your proposal is good to go. Now don't forget the necessary attachments. Again, check the donor's guidelines.

Cover letter This is a very brief description of the proposal, signed by the executive director. It should be a page or page-and-a-half long. (See page 158 for how to create one.)

Cover page State the name of your project. At the bottom put your organization's name, address, and phone number, and the executive director's name.

Table of contents List the proposal sections and attachments with their corresponding page numbers.

The proposal This is the entire proposal, including a budget summary. It includes a list of key personnel and board members.

Line-item budget This is a detailed breakdown of expenses and revenue, section by section.

Letters of endorsement Attach copies of your letters of recommendation from political and community leaders.

Press clips If your proposal refers to newspaper or other clippings that describe your organization and its work, include copies of them.

Copy of organization's 501(c) 3 letter This shows that any money given to you by the funder is going to a group that is a legal nonprofit organization. (Grant proposals for individuals do not need this document.)

Delivery: The Earlier, the Better

If you can, send your proposal by regular mail to arrive early, before the deadline. The earlier it arrives, the sooner the staff can begin looking at it. They'll also have time to offer you tips on making your proposal better or to warn you about a missing document. The U.S. Postal Service offers Priority Mail for oversize packages for under $5; it takes two to three days for delivery. Check to see if the donor allows overnight mail delivery.

Avoid these top six delivery mistakes:

1. **Mistake:** Sending your proposal overnight so you can work on it until the last minute.

   Why: Last-minute editing usually creates mistakes. You must always factor in time for proofreading your proposal.

2. **Mistake:** Sending your proposal by messenger.

   Why: The funders will think you waste money. They like to give funds to money managers who can make it go further and serve more people.

3. **Mistake:** Dropping off your proposal in person on the deadline day.

   Why: If you have to work right up to the last minute to get your proposal done, the foundation will think you are not organized. Of course, there are always exceptions and you might be one, but why risk it?

4. **Mistake:** Faxing it.

   Why: It's easier to read original pages and hard to read faxed pages. Faxed pages may get separated.

5. **Mistake:** E-mailing it.

   Why: The funder may not have the right software to open it. If they do, it puts the burden on them to print it out. And there is no way of checking that their printout is correct.

6. **Mistake:** Forgetting to call to confirm the funder received the package.

   Why: Call after about 10 days to make sure your package arrived. If it didn't, you can send out another. If it did, you've made a good, brief, caring first impression. Plus, if the program officer has questions and wants to talk about your project, this is a great opportunity for you to win an advocate. Be prepared with your script and project file handy. Be brief, direct, and friendly. Your smile and your passion should be evident over the phone. (See page 162 for more on following up.)

following up

Build good relationships

Waiting to hear whether you made the cut can be stressful. On average, it takes about two months—and sometimes much longer—to hear from a funder about the success or failure of the proposal. While you are waiting, you can do a few proactive things. For starters, 10 to 14 days after you've mailed your proposal, call the funder to make sure it arrived. If you have spoken with the program director before (see page 140), ask to speak to her again. Once you get her on the phone and have learned that your proposal is there and under review, ask if this is a good time for a couple of quick questions, then ask the following:

■ **Is the decision-making process on schedule?** Mention the date you understand the decision is to be made and ask if the program officer can verify it. Timetables may have changed for many reasons.

■ **Do you need any additional information?** Once the program officer or reviewing committee has looked over the proposal, they may want more background on your personnel, your organization's history, or any statistics you may have cited in the proposal. Offer to mail any needed information immediately. Or they may just want you to call back in a few weeks to answer a couple of questions over the phone.

■ **Would a meeting with our executive director and project director be helpful?** If yes, the meeting might include a tour of your site. (See page 164 for more information on setting up a meeting.)

Remember, donors like to give money to causes and to people that make them feel comfortable. Strike a balance somewhere between being pushy and being reserved. If you are helping the donor by bringing them exactly the kind of project they are looking to support, your confidence will radiate.

SK THE EXPERTS

Can I e-mail instead of calling to find out if the proposal arrived and if other information is needed?

Unless the program officer asked you to e-mail, it is better to call. You're trying to build a relationship, and your voice can convey more than an e-mail can. Save e-mail until you've established some rapport.

What about following up by mail?

At this stage, no, you want to call to be sure they received your package. If additional information is required, use special delivery mail. Call back to confirm that they received that package, too.

FIRST PERSON DISASTER STORY
Keep Everyone in the Loop

I drafted the proposal for the after-school program, then my executive director looked it over and made a few fixes. She didn't have time to really read it. But she had to sign the cover letter because she's the person responsible for the program, and her phone number appeared as the one to call for more information. She had not been very involved with developing the proposal. When she got a call from the program officer at the foundation asking why we had so many hours budgeted for the bus drivers, she couldn't give an answer. A few weeks later, when I called the program officer to ask if any additional information was needed, I found out they were still waiting for her to get back to them. I quickly had a session with my boss to review the proposal in more detail and gave her my home number so I could help her with any questions that might come up. But it was too late. We didn't get the grant. Next time, we'll keep each other better informed.

—Glenda K., El Paso, Texas

planning a meeting

Make sure
everyone is on
the same page

Great news—the funder has called your executive director and asked to have a meeting to go over the grant project. The funder will usually specify the place and length of the meeting. It can be anything from a 10-minute meeting in the foundation office to a full-blown on-site presentation.

What's a funder looking for at the meeting? Here are a few points they may want to explore.

- **Is the personnel up to the job?** Your executive director and possibly the program director should be able to talk in depth about the organization's history, current programs, and the program that is a candidate for funding.

- **Can the program overcome problems?** The prospective donor might want to ask the executive director and the director of the project about problems that have traditionally plagued programs such as the one you are contemplating. Think through possible approaches in advance so your director can answer easily.

- **Is the organization having a positive impact in the community it serves?** The funder might want to tour facilities, observe any existing programs in action, and talk to people who benefit from those programs.

- **Is the site adequate for the program?** Foundation staff may ask for a guided tour. If the site will not be available until the program begins, the project director should have detailed plans and pictures of it to demonstrate that it will work just fine.

- **Is the program scalable?** Prepare alternative spending plans in case the donor offers you more or less money than you requested. They want to know you've thought about other possibilities.

Planning the Meeting

It's the job of the executive director or program director to plan the meeting and create an agenda. The grantwriter is usually not present unless he will be working on the project once it is funded. The grant writer is like a midwife—once the goods are delivered, the job is done.

■ **Name the attendees**   Only people who will be working in the program should attend. The executive director and program director should attend the meeting, plus anyone else the prospective funder asks to meet. If a board member is especially interested in the project, she might be a valuable person to have at the meeting.

■ **Find out who will be there from the potential funder**   Get the names of those who will attend from the foundation's program officer. Try to find out (on your own) everything you can about them—background, role in the donor organization, past program interests, even favorite vacation spots. Then write a quick brief about them for the people who will attend from your organization. This could help prevent your people from talking down to foundation staff or others about already familiar data. Plus, they will have some points to use for making conversation.

■ **Prepare the agenda**   Decide which points you want to emphasize about the program. (The donor's program officer may be able to help you by explaining what the donor's staff will want to talk about.) Write down the points that should be covered, then practice the presentation with your executive director and program director. If possible, create charts and other visuals to help focus the discussion. Make sure each of your representatives has a role and knows which points to cover. Forward a copy of the agenda to the attending funder.

■ **Emphasize how the program meets the funder's priorities**   Brief your colleagues on this donor's stated mission, their funding guidelines, and any grants the donor has given to others. Make sure they know exactly what the proposal has said about how your program will fulfill these needs and the needs of the community it serves.

now what do I do?

Answers to common questions

Why should our executive director sign the cover letter and the letter of intent? After all, I'm the one writing them.

The executive director is the person responsible for your organization, and therefore for all the projects it runs. Your proposal-writing contribution should be considered a draft for the executive director's use. The only time this might not be the case is when you yourself will be running a program, but the sponsoring organization will receive the funding for you because you do not have 501(c)3 status (see pages 26–31).

How can I get help from our board members on funding? A couple of our members know people who are on the boards of foundations.

Your own board members can be helpful to you, but only if the foundations where they have contacts are funding programs such as the one you are proposing. In certain situations, however, board members may recuse themselves from making such an appeal if the foundation has rules against it. If you do ask a board member to speak to someone at a foundation on behalf of the project, be sure to tell your executive director and project director of your request. They need to be kept in the loop about every effort that is made on behalf of the project.

Can I send my proposal "return receipt requested"?

Sure. If the package was lost and there was a deadline, it is helpful to have proof of when it was sent.

One foundation asks for proposals to be typed only in Courier typeface, and another wants Times Roman. Why these strict rules about how the proposal should look?

The foundation committees want the proposal to be easy for them to read. They are accustomed to certain styles, and it is best to follow their guidelines. For instance, if they want you to fill out a form rather than sending in a formal proposal, that is exactly what you should do. The reason is that they want to look in the same place for the same information in every application. The closer you can come to perfect adherence to all regulations in your application and proposal, the better your chances of acceptance.

Now Where Do I Go?

CONTACTS

The Foundation Center
www.fdncenter.org

BOOKS

Demystifying Grant Seeking:
What You Really Need to Do to Get Grants
By Larissa Golden Brown and
Martin John Brown

Secrets of Successful Grantsmanship:
A Guerrilla Guide to Raising Money
By Susan L. Golden

The Complete Guide to Getting a Grant:
How to Turn Your Ideas Into Dollars
By Laurie Blum

The Foundation Center's Guide to Proposal
Writing, 3rd Edition
By Jane C. Geever and Patricia McNeill

Getting feedback

you got the grant!

Say thank you

You got it! The grant money is yours for your very noble and worthwhile project. Good for you! Of course, since this is grant-world, the first thing you need to do is write a thank-you letter to your new benefactor. They love hearing how happy they make people. And it will build on your new relationship.

In your letter, let them know that they can come to visit the project in action anytime they want. Your words should strive to make them feel welcome and let them know that by giving funds, they are valued members of your organizational family. Use warm, specific language. Avoid cloying sentimentality.

Note: Be sure to use the exact wording the funder uses when referring to your grant. The wording may differ from your own name for the project because, with funders working on many projects with similar titles, they often give each its own special name.

Add the names of the key people at the foundation to your newsletter mailing list, your holiday greeting card list, and the invitation list to special events for your project or organization.

FIRST PERSON DISASTER STORY
It Was Only a Press Release

We were so glad to get a grant for our medical research project that the public relations department put out a press release right away. The very next day, the program director from the foundation called, furious, saying that we had given false information in the release about why we were awarded the grant. It seems we had implied that the funds were part of the foundation's medical awards. As it turned out, the most significant aspect of our proposal as far as the foundation was concerned was the fact that graduate students would run the experiments, and that made it fit the foundation's mission in educational aid. Talk about starting off on the wrong foot! We learned too late that we should never send out a press release referring to a funder before getting it reviewed and approved by them.

—Gloria L., Little Rock, Arkansas

Sample Thank-you Letter

ANY MUSIC SCHOOL · 445 Dream Street · Chicago, IL 00000

September 29, 2002

Mr. Roger Ellis
WRS Foundation
775 Goodwill Avenue
Chicago, IL 00000

Dear Mr. Ellis:

Name of project (as it appears in the award letter)

We are deeply grateful for your gift of $15,000 in support of the project to expand the Family Music Workshop Scholarship Fund. Your generosity will enable us to double the number of families we are able to accept for the family piano workshops, while ensuring that our selection more closely reflects the diversity of the people who live in our community. Without your help, many of our local families would never be able to give any sort of musical instruction to their children.

Anticipated results

Using this gift from the WRS Foundation, we anticipate accepting some 30 new families into the workshops. We will also be able to offer a new piano scholarship for the year to a promising student who is identified in the workshops.

Invitation to visit project

You will be receiving an invitation to the annual student recital in June. Meanwhile, we would be delighted to welcome you or another representative from the WRS Foundation to visit our facilities and observe the family piano workshops or sit in on one of the private lessons. If you wish to make such arrangements, please do not hesitate to contact me at 000-000-0000.

Evaluation plans and reporting schedule

We will evaluate the progress of the new families in the piano workshop at the end of each quarter and send you reports detailing their progress. We will also forward a biography of the scholarship student and the teacher's analysis showing how the student was chosen. We will send you a complete report at the end of the funding period. Meanwhile, if you have any questions, please do not hesitate to contact me.

Sincerely yours,

Gabrielle Jorgens

Gabrielle Jorgens
Executive Director

if the answer is no

Find out why

You got turned down. It's okay. It happens far more often than not. In fact, more than half of all grant proposals are rejected. Don't despair; your effort was as noble as your cause. The only constructive thing to do is learn why it happened.

Wait a week after receiving your letter of rejection, until your spirits are a little brighter, then call the program officer and ask if she could give you some constructive criticism. Some may not have the time, but from those who do, you'll learn a lot.

Note: The program officer is not the person who makes the final decision about a grant; she may have even favored your proposal and defended it during the decision-making process.

Use these tips when talking with a program officer.

■ **Be polite**   This is not the time for ax-grinding. In fact, it's a good idea to start the conversation off by thanking the program officer for taking the time to review your proposal and talk with you about it.

■ **Ask her to tell you briefly how and why your proposal was turned down**   This is not the time to defend your project or your writing.

■ **Resist the urge to argue**   Listen quietly and intently, and write down what she says.

■ **Ask if you might revise your proposal and apply again during the next application cycle**   (Some funders do not take repeat applications, while others encourage them.)

■ **Ask if she is aware of any other funding sources that might be more suitable for your project**   Don't try to persuade her to change the decision.

■ **Send a note thanking her for her time.**   Tell her your organization will reapply (if appropriate).

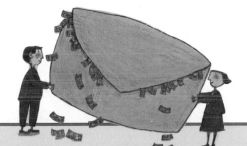

Five Reasons Grant Proposals Get Rejected

1. The donor ran out of money Foundations want to put their funds in many different places, usually on a project basis, in hopes of helping a number of causes instead of just a few. They have only a certain amount to give each year, so while your project was just right for them, they may be short on funds. Find out if that is the case, and if it is, try again next year.

2. The donor wasn't interested You sent your proposal to an inappropriate donor. You need to double-check your research to find those donors who are committed to the same work as your project. Also, grants are often rejected because of donor restrictions. (For more on that, see page 138.) Your proposal's budget may have been to high or to low, or your project may be a high-risk venture. Perhaps your organization and its leadership appeared unstable.

3. You sent proposals to only one or two prospective donors Find more suitable prospects, tailor a proposal to fit each of their missions, make personal contacts, and follow up on every one of those contacts year after year to ensure more funding. Typically, if it's your first time, your rate of acceptance is likely to be low. To increase your odds, you need to get your proposal out to more than one or two funders.

4. Your organization has not yet worked out other ways to raise money Fees, ticket sales, grants from other donors, public giving—there are many ways your project might find money to carry on its work. Many donors are more likely to be interested in helping you if they see that you are pursuing other grants and getting donations from your board and community.

5. Your project is too vague Either your project or your proposal just wasn't strong enough or convincing enough. Donors like to see well-written proposals about well-designed projects.

reporting your results

Quarterly, and again at the end of the grant period

Once the program is under way, the project director will need to send your funder periodic reports on the progress of your program. It keeps them involved in your project.

How often do you report results? As often as the donor requests or depending on your project's time frame. One-year projects should

do a report every quarter. How exactly do you report these results? In a letter, simply state the objectives you have reached thus far and point to ones on the horizon. Use any measurable statistics you can and include real-life examples to humanize your progress. Don't be afraid to report mishaps. Funders are aware that not everything can go according to plan and that you may have some changes to make. If the attendance isn't as high as you had projected, or the test results come up negative over and over, report it, and if you think you can fix the problem, say so.

The report at the end of the grant period (see the sample on the opposite page) can be one or two pages long and accompanied by copies of statistical documents if the project is technical. Follow a similar but more concise format for quarterly reports. Some donors will ask for a financial statement of how the money was spent.

Sample Progress Report

ANY MUSIC SCHOOL · 445 Dream Street · Chicago, IL 00000

June 27, 2003

Mr. Roger Ellis
WRS Foundation
775 Goodwill Avenue
Chicago, IL 00000

First-name basis
(If that has developed)

Dear Roger:

Name of project
(exactly as It appears
In the award letter so
the funder will
recognize it)

Thanks to the generous gift of $15,000 from the WRS Foundation in support of the project to expand the Family Music Workshop Scholarship Fund, during the past nine months we have been able to offer two new workshops with 15 families participating in each one. At the end of the term, 28 families were still participating. (The 2 who dropped out have moved away from the community.)

Ethnic representation in our workshops has improved to 35% African-American, 12% Hispanic, and 8% Asian-American. Interest and appreciation for classical music have grown to the extent that two-thirds of the families in the workshops have taken their children to the Saturday Children's Concert Series at least once during the season (with free tickets obtained through the public schools).

Summarize results

Our new scholarship student, chosen from the children who came with their parents to the workshops, is Rena Washington, age 8. She is the child of a single mother. Her mother works as a practical nurse with the Visiting Nurse Service of the St. Francis Medical Assistance Program.

The instructor of the workshop attended by Rena and her mother recognized the girl's musical ability during the second session, when she repeated the melodies from classical selections played during the first session by singing them without prompting. After two private mini-lessons indicated Rena's interest was genuine, she was awarded the scholarship. (Fortunately, a gift from the Kawai Foundation allowed us to obtain a used piano for her so that she could practice at home as long as she continues her lessons.) As you heard when you attended the recital earlier this month, her progress shows that she is quite gifted.

Make a possible
appeal
for more funds

Based on the benefits derived from your grant during the past year, we hope, with your continued generosity, to invite a new group of 30 families to participate in family music workshops next fall. Our proposal for that program will be on your desk by the August deadline. Meanwhile, if you have any questions about the results of this past year's expansion of the Family Music Workshop Scholarship Fund, please don't hesitate to call me at 000-000-0000.

Sincerely yours,

Gabrielle Jorgens

Gabrielle Jorgens
Executive Director

asking for more money

Renewing grants, listing past benefactors

A little good news: Some donors like to fund the same project every year or every other year. Once you get your grant money and start building a relationship with the donor, you might ask the program officer at your funding organization about their grant renewal policies. Sometimes donors want to continue funding the same organization, but for different projects. In that case, you'll want to come up with a new project during each funding period. The new project might be an extension or a different aspect of the project that was funded during the previous year.

Even with a donor in your court, it's smart to keep grant proposals going out to a number of different organizations so that your funding is not dependent on just one or two sources. That way, you are more likely to enjoy a steady flow of money.

Deposit the Check

All too often, a check for a grant has been found in the drawer of a director or a board member weeks after it arrived. Sounds unlikely, but it does happen. Maybe the deposit was delayed because a new account needs to be opened for the project, or another staffer was supposed to take care of it and didn't. As the grantwriter, it's a good idea to ask around the office to make sure the check was sent to the bank right away. Otherwise, the check could be canceled automatically after a few weeks. If that happens, it can be hard to get back the money.

 # ASK THE EXPERTS

When should I send a proposal to renew our grant with the same funder?

If your donor does renew funding annually, mention in your final report letter that you will send them a new proposal. If the program officer suggests it, you might even send the proposal for renewed funding along with your final report.

Our donor declined to renew our grant. What should we do?

The natural response is to get angry. Don't. Chances are that your donor ran out of funds. Or, more likely, the donor's policy is to award one-year grants only. Continue to include that funder and every other funder who has helped you on all mailings regarding your organization and send them proposals for new projects. Also, let former funders know about the success of the project and continue to invite them to see the program in action.

keeping in touch

**Build a
network**

When you are awarded grants, grab that chance to work closely
with your funders. Find out what is important to them, and why.
Become acquainted with the people involved; some may turn
into good friends.

As a grantwriter, you will find that as your lists of contacts grow,
you will learn more about the community of donors. You will
come to understand how foundations and other agencies that
donate money work. More important, you will get in on the buzz
of which agency is funding what, and why. This kind of inside
knowledge can make all the difference in winning a grant.

Becoming a Donor

As a grantwriter, your goal is to understand how the philanthropic world works. What better way than to join a group that awards money for good causes? Perhaps your church or community organization will let you sit in on their screening committee. You can see firsthand what the process looks like from the donor's point of view. You will learn how group decisions can vary about which causes to recommend for funding and which to turn down. These observations are likely to help you as you write grant proposals for your own project.

If you think about it, your decisions about your personal giving at year's end also can be instructive. Just notice how you shuffle through the direct appeals that are mailed to you each year. You, too, weigh the types of programs that come closest to your personal interests and the letters and brochures that explain the causes in the most appealing way. Your decision-making about which cause to support is probably very similar to the more formal process that a funding organization uses to consider your proposal.

TIP: You are more likely to get a second gift if you keep in touch and send updates to the donor throughout the year. Funders get "donor fatigue" hearing from organizations only when they want something.

now what do I do?

We were just awarded a grant. Now the donor wants to meet with us. Does this mean we might not get the money?

No, it probably means that the donor wants to go over your proposal in more detail and make sure that your project will be efficiently developed. The donor may have given funds to similar causes and could offer suggestions or ask pertinent questions. Or perhaps this is her first time donating to such a cause, and she wants to find out more about the project. Prepare carefully for the meeting (see page 164) so that you can clarify your plans and explain what you expect to happen over the course of the project.

We were awarded a grant for commissioning new plays for our community theater's summer festival, but we ended up using part of the money to pay for costumes for our winter production when its expenses ran over budget. How should we report this?

This is a difficult situation. You can find yourself in trouble legally. Ethically, you're obligated to offer to return the money, even though you spent it. But check your grant paperwork. Some funders, especially for large grants, allow a percentage of funds to be shifted from one expense to another within the same project and ask to be informed of changes over that amount. In the future, before you make a major change in how you spend a grant, first ask permission of the funder. If you don't, you'll probably lose the option of getting future grants from them. And because funders share information with each other, it could hurt your chances for getting grants from other donors.

Our project developed into a disaster. Nothing turned out the way we projected it. If we report what happened, the funders will think their money was wasted. Should we fudge the results?

Never lie to the funder about what has happened, no matter how bad things turn out. Of course, you want to present things in the best light possible, but there is no harm in suggesting what might have made the program better and therefore what you might want to change for the next year. For instance, you might ask for more money to advertise the program or more training for the project staff.

Who makes these decisions about grant awards anyway?

Each funding group is different. If you have applied to a small family foundation, a single member of the family may review the proposals after her staff has screened them. Many large foundations have a committee of board members who review proposals and then present the most pertinent ones to the rest of the board. A big corporate group may behave like a large foundation, but in a small business the decision will probably be made by the owner. A government agency might use a panel of experts or others who are associated with the agency.

We ended up not needing some of the grant money. What should we do with the leftover funds?

You need to contact your donor and ask what they prefer. Be sure to emphasize you met the project's objectives more efficiently than projected. Some may ask for the money back. If it's a small amount, some may let you use it to fund another project. Have project suggestions to offer.

Now Where Do I Go?

CONTACTS

www.loanweb.com

www.bankrate.com

BOOKS

How Foundations Work
By Dennis P. McIlnay

The Five Life Stages of Nonprofit Organizations: Where You Are, Where You're Going, and What to Expect When You Get There
By Judith Sharken Simon and Terence J. Donovan

appendix

Sample Letter of Intent

GROWING GREAT READERS PROJECT • Thursdon Hills Elementary School P. O. Box 2722 • Thursdon Hills, GA 00000

June 10, 2003

Robert Bailey
Executive Director
Avon Humanities Foundation
108 Centre Avenue, Suite 115
Thursdon Hills, GA 00000

Dear Mr. Bailey:

Problem
Over the last year the Parent Teachers Association at Thursdon Hills Elementary School has become concerned about our first graders' reading scores. Over half the children in first grade cannot read at grade level at the end of the school year. Yet the reading levels can be improved with tutoring, which is currently available only to a few of our Thursdon Hills students who are from affluent families.

Solution
To improve these reading scores the PTA is establishing an educational project called Growing Great Readers. With support from Avon Humanities Foundation we will create a program using volunteers from the local retirement home as tutors to improve the reading scores of our first graders.

Goal
Our goal is to enroll as many of our 50 first-grade children in the tutoring sessions as possible. Promotions, including media releases and TV appearances, will advertise the Growing Great Readers project in the community.

How it will be accomplished
A professional reading consultant will direct our Growing Great Readers Project. She will confer with the first-grade teachers at Thursdon Hills Elementary School in order to coordinate the project's tutoring program with their lesson plans. The director will then train our community tutors—approximately 30 volunteers drawn from the Richardson Hills Retirement Community (across the street from the Thursdon Hills Elementary School).

We will appeal to the parents of our students to attend evening workshops, where they will be instructed in how to support their child's reading efforts at home. The sessions will emphasize different aspects of reading readiness.

Evaluation

To keep the Avon Humanities Foundation apprised of the progress of our project, we will send regular reports and evaluations. In the fall we will send a report on enrollment—of both students and teachers—in the Growing Great Readers tutorial sessions and workshops. Every three months we will send attendance records. If you or other representatives from the Avon Humanities Foundation want to observe the training sessions, the tutorial programs or the parent workshops, you would be most welcome.

At the end of the school term, a complete report will be submitted comparing the Thursdon Hills Elementary School first-grade scores for the current year with those from the previous year and with those from other schools in the state. Summaries of reactions from both parents and teachers will be included.

History of your organization

Founded in 1988, the Thursdon Hills Elementary School PTA is dedicated to the continual improvement of the learning experience for every child in the school. It coordinates the efforts of the children's parents with those of their teachers in carrying out programs that can bring about such improvement. Since its inception, the PTA has raised $175,000 in funds and in-kind donations for such projects as parent workshops on how to help with homework; teacher-upgrade seminars in reading, science, math and art; and field trips for the students to museums and performing arts events.

Other funding

The Thursdon Hills Elementary School PTA receives its operating expenses from public funds allotted by the state legislature. Its other program expenses come mainly from parent membership donations (60% of the parents are members of the PTA; of those, 80% are donors). Local businesses have been most generous in their support of the PTA programs, primarily with in-kind donations of computers, VCR's and furnishings. Other funds come from special events such as bake sales and garage sales.

Conclusion and summary

With a generous grant of $45,000 from the Avon Humanities Foundation, we will address the substandard reading performance of our children in the Thursdon Hills Elementary School with our Growing Great Readers project. Your grant will go toward training our volunteer tutors to coach our first graders in a way that will enhance their teachers' efforts. We will advise our parents how to optimize the children's reading experiences at home. These efforts will help our students establish a foundation in reading skills, enabling them to perform better in every subject throughout their school years.

Contact

Thank you for your consideration. With your permission we will forward a full proposal. If you have any questions, please don't hesitate to call me at at 000-000-0000.

Sincerely yours,

Signature *Virginia Loomis*

Virginia Loomis
Project Chairman

Sample Grant Proposal 1

This is a real, grant-winning proposal. The names and places have been changed to protect the privacy of the parties involved. The format differs from the samples in chapter 3. If you have any doubts about which format to use, follow the prospective donor's guidelines. Below is an example of a grant proposal based on information the donor requested in its application form.

Request for Support to Roper Finance Foundation for The Health and Welfare Cooperative's Year 2002 Expansion Project

Background Information on the Organization

History and Mission   The Health and Welfare Cooperative of Laurence-ville was founded in 1988 as a nonprofit organization, run by local volunteers. Its mission is to raise funds to provide financial assistance to people in Laurenceville who are in danger of becoming homeless due to job loss, medical bills, or other crises.

The Health and Welfare Cooperative receives funds from concerned friends and neighbors, civic groups, clubs, churches, temples, and businesses. This year we are seeking grants, since more families than ever need assistance.

At The Health and Welfare Cooperative, we understand that many families need a helping hand at one time or another. Our intervention of temporary financial assistance and counseling can prevent a family from having to move or a senior citizen from having to leave their home of many years.

Funds raised by The Health and Welfare Cooperative are utilized efficiently— 92 cents out of every dollar raised is given to Laurenceville Association, Inc., whose professional staff utilize the funds to help qualified Laurenceville residents in danger of losing their homes.

Here is an example of a family we recently helped.

A Family in Need   A single mother, in her mid-forties and with two children, works and rents out an apartment upstairs in her home, in addition to taking care of her invalid sister. Her tenants did not pay rent for three months; she in turn fell behind on her mortgage and was facing foreclosure. Laurenceville Association contacted the mortgage company and made arrangements to pay the outstanding debt. Foreclosure was avoided, the family remained together in their home, and the children kept their schools, friends, and social support systems.

The Health and Welfare Cooperative's goal is to keep families together in their homes in Laurenceville, in addition to being a consistent source of hope and support for people in despair. The Health and Welfare Cooperative is assisting families in maintaining their homes and keeping families in their homes and intact for humanitarian reasons—because we care. By keeping Laurenceville families from being displaced, continuity, a healthy customer base, property values, and a sound community are maintained.

Current Programs, 2001 Activities, and Most Recent Significant Accomplishments   The Health and Welfare Cooperative's current programs consist of a variety of special events and projects designed to raise funds and make the public aware of the needs of the neediest among us.

2001 activities include an annual Townwide Garage Sale, a Pasta Night at Patsy's Pizza restaurant, a Cut-a-Thon at Glorianna Salon, a Ladies Night Out, several Penny Drives in conjunction with local merchants, an annual mailing, and a variety of social get-togethers attended by town leaders. The Health and Welfare Cooperative also assists the Laurenceville Club with their annual House Tour.

Names/Titles/Years of Service of Senior Staff; Number and Function of Paid, Full-time Staff; Part-time Staff; Volunteers   The Health and Welfare Cooperative of Laurenceville is a 100% volunteer organization totaling 18 board members and 3 directors emeritus.

Request for Support to Roper Finance Foundation

The Health and Welfare Cooperative of Laurenceville is seeking $5,000 from the Roper Finance Foundation for the The Health and Welfare Cooperative Year 2002 Expansion Project, which will enable us to serve an additional 10 local families facing housing crises.

A. Statement of Primary Purpose and Need/Problem in 2001   The Health and Welfare Cooperative raised $17,200, which was put to use helping 19 families (59 children and adults) with an average amount of $900 per family (typically, two or three partial mortgage payments).

Unfortunately, not everyone who required assistance received it. In 2002, we would like to be able to support a greater number of families who request assistance. The purpose of this project is to help 10 additional families, enabling us to assist a total of 30 families in the coming year.

B. Population to Be Served Currently The Health and Welfare Cooperative serves primarily single mothers with school-age children and senior citizens on fixed incomes living in Laurenceville.

C. Strategies to Implement the Project The Health and Welfare Cooperative encourages neighborhood awareness and community investment in low-income housing through a multifaceted strategy of local community fund-raising, repeat activities, and an annual mailing. These events brought us $17,200 during the last fiscal year, but The Health and Welfare Cooperative needs additional funds. This is why we are embarking upon a proposal-writing campaign, requesting grants of $5,000 to $10,000 from foundations and corporations like Roper Finance Foundation. Our goal is to raise an additional $10,000 through this effort.

D. Itemized Project Budget Funds raised are given to the Laurenceville Association for disbursement to those in the community who are in immediate and urgent need.

E. Collaborative Projects or Partnerships with Other Organizations
Addressing similar issues in our service area, The Health and Welfare Cooperative of Laurenceville helps to financially support the Laurenceville Association, Inc. The Health and Welfare Cooperative assists the Laurenceville Club with their annual House Tour in return for a portion of the proceeds. The Health and Welfare Cooperative organizes and conducts many other fund-raising activities within the community. We work closely with local houses of worship as well as concerned local businesses, such as the First Federal Bank, General Grocery, Bowen Shoe Manufacturing, and Front Street Insurance Company, who all recognize the need for community investment and donate goods, services, food, and space.

F. Specific Outcome as the Measure of Success   Our Year 2002 Expansion Project will be deemed a success if we raise sufficient funds to assist an additional 10 families, bringing our total annual clients served to 30.

Conclusion

We hope that Roper Finance Foundation will be able to make a contribution of $5,000 in support of our efforts to expand. Together we can make an important investment in our community. Please call me at 000-000-0000 if you require additional information. Thank you for considering this request.

Sincerely,

Ira Goodfellow

Ira Goodfellow
Executive Director

Sample Grant Proposal 2

This is a real, grant-winning proposal. The names and places have been changed to protect the privacy of the parties involved. The format differs from the samples in chapter 3. If you have any doubts about which format to use, follow the prospective donor's guidelines.

Grant Renewal Proposal to The Maldive Foundation for General Program Support

March 2002

Submitted by:
Lou Barber and Val Lupone
Artistic Directors
Lookout Theater
856 West 48th Street
New York, NY 10000

Contact:
Joseph Lincoln
Director of Development
Telephone: 000-000-0000
Fax: 000-000-0000
E-mail: Joel@lookouttheater.org

Introduction

When we founded Lookout Theater, our mission was simple: to present new theatrical voices to New York audiences. For eight years, Lookout Theater has accomplished this through three interrelated programs: our four-play season committed to New York and world premieres has made us an Off-Broadway leader and one of the most exciting theaters in Manhattan; our Writer's Workshop Department actively seeks new and emerging writers in the theater and nurtures their growth with readings, labs, and workshops; and our School Liaison Department brings theater to New York City schools, allowing more than 1,200 students each year to find new ways to learn, increase literacy, and discover their own voices in the arts.

Lookout Theater carries out this mission because we believe in the artist as the primary force in creating memorable theater. We believe each experience in the theater should be an event where artists in playwriting, acting, direction, and design combine to compel the audience to have an emotional reaction, getting them personally involved in the production at hand. We feel that this is best done with new work, which allows the audience to hear new voices and perspectives that can mingle with the audience's own experiences, resulting in a fresh discovery of the world around them and creating a dialogue that continues long after the curtain falls. To facilitate this new work, we envision our theater as a home where theatrical artists are empowered to do their best by giving them artistic freedom, a strong sense of community, and full institutional support.

As a small theater, we are able to take risks on plays that the commercial theater often ignores. Some of our biggest successes were rejected by nearly every other theater in Manhattan. Hannah Longstreet's "Holding Space Back," Georgina Flores' "Beyond Rio," Gregor Janosec's current "New at the Art of Fooling": These are tough, engrossing plays that investigate the issues and morality of our times. Over the years, this dedication to the work of new and emerging artists has earned us a variety of awards. Ms. Longstreet's "Holding Space Back" transferred to a larger theater for a long commercial run. Indeed, many of our plays have been subsequently produced around the world, enriching the theatrical canon with substantive plays. With each season, the impressive list of artists who work at our intimate 99-seat theater continues to grow. In the 2003–2004 season, we will feature another of Ms. Longstreet's plays, actor/director Gunnar Fogelsen, award-winning actress Sherry Upton, director Lee Pei, and award-winning actor/director Harvey Levenstein side by side with two new writers, Retha Summers and Nathaniel Bloom.

As an organization, we have grown tremendously. In 1998, we employed one full-time staff member and two part-time staff, with an operating budget of $465,000. Today, we have six full-time staff and three part-time staff, with an operating budget of over $1,500,000—plus a growing subscription audience entering its third year and a robust individual donor program. With such strong administrative and institutional support in place, our programs are in turn reaching more people than ever. We are extremely excited about our 2001–2002 season.

Mainstage Season

Lookout Theater believes that new plays are the cornerstone of American theater, and we are dedicated to presenting an array of voices—from the comic to the searing—that commercial theater often ignores. By presenting this diversity of viewpoints and styles on our stage, we make the theater a relevant source of social and emotional dialogue. In this tradition, we are marking our ninth season with a stirring mix of New York, American, and world premieres that are distinct and fresh representatives of American playwriting as we begin the 21st century. (See Attachments for details.)

Lookout's audience for these exciting plays is largely drawn from the five boroughs of New York City, as well as New Jersey and Connecticut. Our audience constituency is considerably affected by the subject matter and key ethnicity of the plays. However, Lookout is committed to bringing the rich diversity of New York's population together. Through targeted marketing and subsidized ticket offerings, we actively seek to bring underserved and minority audiences into our theater. These initiatives have expanded our reach into the diverse New York community and attracted a wide cross-section of new and returning audiences.

Literary Programs

Lookout Theater's commitment to new work extends far beyond our mainstage season. Lookout Theater has implemented a series of programs to nurture emerging theatrical voices.

Writer's Workshop Department   In the fall of 2000, the workshop manager invited 18 burgeoning playwrights from the thousands who send scripts to Lookout Theater to join the workshop. This group meets at Lookout Theater once every two weeks to support and develop the craft of its member writers through discussion, criticism, readings, and collaborative projects. Workshop members are using this invaluable forum to develop their plays, test their ideas, and share experiences in a supportive and insightful environment.

While this forum is flexible enough to change and evolve according to each playwright's needs, the meetings currently focus on their works in progress and new ideas. A basic structure is in place which allows each playwright at least 30 minutes each meeting to use as they wish: read a scene, work on an outline, and/or ask the group for feedback to help determine the best dramatic path for a play. The time devoted to the participants may be longer, depending on how many wish to discuss their work on a given evening. The intention is to create a healthy group mentorship that benefits all members. Now grown to 15 members, the workshop represents a wide spectrum of styles, from lyrical writers to harsh urban voices. This diversity is intended to create an enriching environment in which members will be informed of other means of dramatic expression very different from their own and have the opportunity to learn from each other's strengths.

Periodically, each playwright from the workshop will choose one of their completed new plays to be read in the monthly Sound-off. At each Sound-off, up to three plays may be read on successive Monday evening events that are open to the public. Playwrights, actors, directors, and audience members can meet one another in a relaxed, social setting, offering important feedback to the writer's work. This informal atmosphere also gets the members out of the solitude of the writer's world and encourages networking with other theatrical artists. Through the Sound-off series, important relationships between artists form, creating new work and partnerships that extend beyond Lookout Theater to the larger theatrical community.

Discovery Readings   After a play has been crafted in a workshop, it can be recommended for a Discovery Reading. Discovery Readings are unstaged readings by professional actors of new plays that are under consideration for the Lookout Theater mainstage season and are open to all writers. Because of the live nature of theater, these readings are a chance for the artistic directors of Lookout Theater to hear a play as it is meant to be heard. Open to the public, these readings also provide important exposure for the playwrights to the larger New York City theater community.

Studio Series   After these initial readings, a play that shows unrealized potential might be worked on in Lookout Theater's Studio Series. The writer works with a director, professional actors, and members of the Lookout Theater Writer's Workshop Department to develop the shape, scope, and content of the piece. During one or two intensive weeks of reading and rewrites, the author receives important feedback from the artistic team, culminating in a staged reading. This is often an invaluable period of development of a play, where the playwright can hear and rework his play with the full support of professionals at the top of their craft. It is the hope that after this significant time of growth, the play will be ready for inclusion in the next Lookout Theater mainstage season.

By nurturing work through these programs, we look to provide a theatrical home to playwrights who have not yet found commercial success or public recognition, a place where they can have their plays heard, workshopped, and eventually produced.

School Liaison Department

Lookout Theater has long been at the forefront of education initiatives and progressive techniques. Now in its eighth year, the School Liaison Department has created a curriculum of classroom initiatives that reaches more than 1,200 high school students and their families. In addition, our after-school programs and events held at our theater touch individuals drawn from all walks of life and from all sectors of New York's richly diverse population.

Classroom Partnership Programs   At Lookout Theater, we believe that theater and theatrical techniques are effective tools with which to engage young minds and allow them to explore and interact with the world around them. Acting, improvisation, movement, script analysis, and other skills allow students to become intrinsically and emotionally involved in curriculum from the inside out. Using theater takes the lesson out of the textbook into a world of practical interaction, allowing the student a new and invigorating perspective on the material. Moreover, studying through the arts allows our students, most of whom are from diverse cultural and ethnic backgrounds, to find a common language with which to communicate. By creating this dialogue, theater techniques foster understanding of both the differences and similarities among cultures and peoples.

In our School Enrichment Programs, teaching artists go into New York City classrooms, using theatrical techniques to infuse teachers and students with a more meaningful and interactive learning experience. Currently, we have teaching artists collaborating with teachers in the following New York City high schools: Louis Latimer Academy, Bay Shore School, Hinkel-Flannery School, Ludwig Harrison High School, and Marchand High School. These teaching teams explore a wide range of curriculums with theater techniques, including history, Spanish, and mathematics. Also included are student matinees of appropriate plays at Lookout Theater, accompanied by study guides and pre- and post-performance discussions with teaching artists and members of the artistic team.

Student Outreach Programs   While theater can be an effective means of attaining curriculum-based educational goals, it is also a worthwhile end unto itself. Through our after-school Student Outreach Programs, we immerse students in the study and production of theater, allowing them to master complex artistic and social skills as part of a theatrical community. Our intensive programs are an alternative to the city streets for New York City high school students with an active interest in theater. These pre-professional programs result in life experiences that foster critical thinking skills students can use in any subsequent profession.

Through our Teen Rush Company, students are engaged in all aspects of theater: writing, performing, directing, design, and production. This work culminates in June when the company performs an original theater piece created during the year on the Lookout Theater stage. Summerfest, now in its fourth year, offers New York City high school playwrights the opportunity to develop their plays with professional actors and directors, then see them performed on our stage. In our intensive Theater Prep Program, students choose an artistic discipline and undergo mentorship from professionals for a total of 18 hours each. Students accompany actors, casting directors, playwrights, and directors to learn about their daily lives and the reality of being a professional in the arts. Together, these programs allow young people to discover their voice in the arts, connect Lookout Theater to our community, and expose new audiences to theater. The Education and Outreach Department deals with the widest possible cross-section of New York's community. The program's ethnic breakdown is 29% Hispanic, 26% African-American, 26% Caucasian, 12% Asian-American, and 7% Caribbean, with over 800 young people served.

Conclusion

As our many programs and visibility have grown, so have our organizational costs. The Lookout Theater operating budget for 2003–2004 is $1,520,000. The cost of mounting productions continues to rise, and the need to support emerging talent and arts in education increases every year. Our important Writer's Workshop and School Liaison programs do not generate earned income but represent Lookout Theater's investment in the talent and the audiences of the future. We expect ticket sales and other income to generate $810,000. The additional $710,000 to produce our ninth season must be raised from individuals, corporations, government sources, and foundations.

Now is a particularly exciting time to become a supporter of Lookout Theater. We are currently looking for a new, larger home which will allow us to take the next step in our growth. While our current home at the 99-seat 48th Street Theater is wonderfully intimate, it also limits both the scope of plays we can attempt and the size of audience we can reach. We are currently in negotiations for several spaces, all of which will significantly increase our playing space and audience capacity. In our new home, we will be able to paint on a bigger theatrical canvas and firmly establish ourselves as the premier Off-Broadway showcase for new plays.

With an increased grant of $7,000, the Maldive Foundation would be assuring the continuation of our theater company, helping us to fulfill our mission of presenting new theatrical voices to New York audiences. It is also an investment in the arts of New York City at a time when it is needed the most. We hope you will continue to help!

glossary

Agent
A term that is sometimes used to designate a non-profit, philanthropic organization receiving donations from individuals, foundations, and/or . government agencies.

Annual report
A document published by a foundation or a corporation that describes the details of its financial circumstances and the projects that make up the total of its charitable giving.

Application form
A rigid grant proposal format indicating exactly how a foundation or a government agency wants information to be presented when a nonprofit organization is applying for a grant. It requires more filling in blanks than writing descriptive narrative.

Articles of incorporation
A legal document that sets out the parameters of a nonprofit organization as part of its application to become a nonprofit corporation. Incorporation requirements differ from state to state.

Assets
Resources that are available to a foundation. Assets are often invested in stocks, bonds, and real estate, and their earnings are used for grants. Usually the annual amount of charitable giving must amount to a certain percentage of the total assets. Assets forming a permanent interest-producing fund are referred to as an endowment.

Beneficiary
The person or organization that receives a grant from a foundation, corporation, individual, or government agency.

Building grant
A grant that is awarded to pay for a building or a construction project that will benefit a nonprofit organization.

Call report
A report made by a representative or employee of a nonprofit organization describing any contact with a donor or potential donor. Copies of the report are distributed to the rest of the officers and staff of the organization so that everyone will be able to respond to questions that may be posed to them by the donor.

Campaign
An organized drive for funding conducted by a non-profit organization for a specific period of time for a special purpose. A campaign usually targets individuals. It may utilize several fund-raising methods, such as events, direct mail, and personal appeals by officers and trustees. A campaign may benefit the organization as a whole or a specific aspect of the organization, such as an endowment, a building fund, or a particular project.

Capital support
Grants that are given to an organization for capital expenses, such as a building program, permanent equipment, large-scale construction, or an endowment.

Challenge grant
See **Matching grant**.

Clients
The population served by a nonprofit organization. The term is usually applied to people with health needs or people who are indigent.

Collaborative project
A project that is sponsored by two or more donors in tandem. May also be referred to as a **cooperative project**.

Community foundation
A foundation that gives grants to philanthropic causes within a specific geographic area, usually funded by a donor or donors within that area.

Conference grant
A grant made for the purpose of organizing and managing a conference or seminar to benefit a philanthropic cause. A conference grant may also be awarded to send officers of a nonprofit organization to a similar conference or seminar.

Concept paper
See **Grant proposal.**

Consultant

An individual or a firm contracted to advise on the management of an organization or on the planning, training, and evaluation phases of a project. The consultant is an expert in a given field. He or she is not an employee of the nonprofit organization but instead acts as an individual contractor and is paid a fee for creating and/or managing certain aspects of a project. Sometimes an individual who brings a project to a nonprofit organization may formalize a connection by consulting on the project.

Consulting grant

A grant that is designated to pay for an expert's assistance for a nonprofit organization or one of its projects.

Continuation grant

A grant that is awarded in successive years. Also known as **continuation funds** or **continuing support grants**.

Cooperative gifts

Donations made to support a project of a nonprofit organization by at least two different grantors. Usually the gifts are arranged to be given in tandem. May also be referred to as **collaborative gifts**.

Corporate foundation

A foundation whose assets come from a portion of its profits. Also known as a **company-sponsored foundation**.

Corporate giving

A donation made directly from corporate funds, without being funneled through a corporate foundation. The donation might come from its advertising budget, its marketing budget, or its discretionary budget and may not have to conform to the tax regulations governing foundations.

Cover letter

A short letter, usually one page, that goes with a grant proposal. Its purpose is to introduce the proposed project, emphasizing how it relates to the purposes of the donor organization.

Director

See **Trustee.**

Directory

A compilation of donors that can be comprehensive or broken down by subject, geographic location, or type of donor. The directory may be printed as a book or periodical, or it may take electronic form as a CD or an online directory. The latter may provide actual links to foundation Web sites.

Distribution committee

The committee at a foundation or government agency that is responsible for reviewing applications and awarding grants. Also known as the **reviewing committee**.

Donor

An individual, a foundation, a corporation, or a government agency that awards grants to philanthropic causes. May also be referred to as a **funder**, a **grantor**, or a **grantmaker**.

Endowment

A pool of funds donated to a nonprofit organization that is invested over a long term, and the interest it produces provides a continuous flow of income for the organization.

Equipment grant

A grant that is awarded to pay for major equipment that is to be used by a nonprofit organization.

Evaluation

The reports sent to a foundation or agency that has awarded a grant. The reports are developed by the recipient nonprofit organization to show at specified intervals how a grant has been used, either describing the outcome of a project or verifying the benefits of the overall utilization of endowment or building funds. A budget update may be included if spending has differed from the budget projections in the application.

Family foundation

A foundation whose assets are donated by a single family.

Fellowship

A grant awarded for higher education, usually for graduate or postgraduate study. A fellowship can sometimes require the recipient to contribute work—either as a teacher, artist, or professional—to the institution where the study is done.

Fiscal sponsor

A nonprofit sponsor limited to funneling funds from a donor to a project. May require a fee.

501(c)3

A classification awarded by the Internal Revenue Service designating an organization as a not-for-profit, tax-exempt operation. Most foundations and individuals are required to restrict their philanthropic giving to organizations with this classification.

Form 990-PF

The annual tax statement filed by each foundation. The Internal Revenue Service requires that the statement be made public. Names of the recipients of all grants awarded by the organization during the year must be listed, with the dollar amounts for each grant.

Foundation

An organization or institution that invests a pool of funds, called its assets, in order to make philanthropic grants from the proceeds. Its assets may come from private individuals, a family, or the profits of a corporation. It is managed by a board of trustees or directors.

Funder

See **Donor.**

Fund-raising event

An event such as a performance, showing, sale, or social event that is organized for the financial benefit of a nonprofit organization. Tickets to the event are usually sold to individuals, and the proceeds are given to the organization. The events may include or consist entirely of the sale of goods donated to the organization.

Goal

A section of a grant proposal following the statement of need. It consists of a brief explanation expressed in general terms of how the project or organization will meet that need.

Government agency

An agency set up by the state, city, or federal government that can make grants to individuals or nonprofit organizations.

Grant proposal

A document used in applying for funding from a foundation, a corporation, a government agency, or an individual donor. Its text, which may be referred to as a narrative, describes a project or an aspect of a nonprofit organization that needs funds. Its length may vary, depending on the guidelines and instructions from the foundation to which it is directed. May also be referred to as a **concept paper** or a **white paper**.

Guidelines

Suggested procedures for filing an application for a grant. Grantseekers who follow the guidelines of a particular foundation or government agency may enjoy a decided advantage when the application is reviewed.

Grantmaker

See **Donor.**

Individual donor

A person who makes a donation to a nonprofit organization and usually obtains a tax deduction as a result.

In-kind donation

A philanthropic donation of goods or services instead of funds. The items or services donated are tax-deductible, based on their monetary value. Goods may include nonpermanent items such as food or flowers or permanent items such as equipment or clothing. Services might range from professional help with taxes to an engineer supervising the installation of a new furnace. Use of real estate without rent is also considered an in-kind donation. In-kind donations are often given by corporations, both large and small, and may be related to their products or services.

Letter of intent

A letter sent by a nonprofit organization to a foundation, consisting of a short version of a formal grant proposal. The letter of intent expresses a desire to send the full-length proposal, provided the foundation response to the short version is positive. May also be called a **query letter**.

Letter of request

A short version of a grant proposal in a letter format. Some foundations stipulate in their guidelines that their grantseekers' applications take this format. It is often used by nonprofit organizations when applying for a continuation grant from a donor with which it has an ongoing relationship.

Loan grant

A grant that is given for a specified time by a foundation or government agency with the intention of having it repaid. A loan grant usually has very low interest, if any.

Marketable product

A product that is made or an event that is produced by a nonprofit organization for the purpose of marketing it to the public. Such products can include tickets to performances or showings, or items that are made to be sold. All profits from such marketing must be retained by the nonprofit organization and used to fund its projects.

Matching grant

A grant that is given to partially fund a project or an organizational budget. The grant does not become available until the amount is matched by gifts from other donors. Matching grants need not be equal, i.e., the same amount from each donor. Instead, a matching grant may stipulate a ratio of 2:1 or 3:1. A variation is the matching gifts some corporations offer their employees. The company will donate an amount to certain philanthropic causes that matches what the employee has given. Also known as a **challenge grant**.

Message board

A section of a Web site where questions may be asked and information may be exchanged.

Mission statement

A statement describing the broad purposes of a nonprofit organization, usually composed as part of its articles of incorporation.

Narrative

The text of a grant proposal. The footnotes at the end of a budget may be referred to as the **budgetary narrative**.

Need

See **Statement of need.**

Nomination

A grant proposal that is sent to a foundation at its own invitation. The invitation is usually issued by a designated committee of nominators. Some foundations request that only those organizations or individuals who have been nominated by their committee submit grant proposals.

Nonprofit organization

An organization dedicated to philanthropic causes and which by law may not engage in any profit-making enterprise unless all revenues are used for those philanthropic causes.

Nonprofit sponsor

An arrangement that allows an individual to obtain nonprofit status for a project by affiliating it to a nonprofit organization through a formal agreement. The organization is able to accept grants for the project and funnel money to it. Control over the project is usually left in the hands of the individual, who may have no other connection with the organization except for possibly sending evaluations back through them to the donors. The organization might share other aspects of the project, such as fund-raising, administrative services, space, and promotion. A fee is usually paid to the nonprofit organization based on the extent of services rendered to the project.

Objectives

The section of a grant proposal that names the two or three concrete targets that a project is designed to reach in order to meet a stated goal. It is usually followed by a detailed description of the program activities, spelling out in detail how the objectives will be met.

Operating foundation

A foundation that is organized for the purpose of operating a project as well as donating the funding for it. It does not give grants to other projects, organizations, or individuals.

Operating grant

A grant given to a nonprofit organization to help defray ordinary annual budget expenses: payroll and personnel benefits, rent or mortgage, utilities and other overhead expenses, plus the costs of the organization's customary activities. Generally, these grants are scarce and therefore difficult to obtain.

Payout requirement

The percentage of a foundation's assets that it is required by law to donate each year to philanthropic causes in the form of grants.

Private foundation

A foundation whose assets come from a private individual or individuals, or a family. It has nonprofit status and is committed to donating to philanthropic causes, usually nonprofit organizations.

Program
See Project.

Program activities

A section of a grant proposal asking for support of a project or a particular need of a nonprofit organization. It explains in detail how the project will accomplish the objectives mentioned earlier in the proposal. May also be referred to as project activities.

Program grant

A grant designed to support a particular project of a nonprofit organization.

Program officer

An employee of a foundation who supervises the application process and the presentation of applications to the distribution committee. Many program officers also manage the grants that are awarded to nonprofit organizations and follow up with evaluations.

Project

An enterprise that is undertaken for a philanthropic purpose. May also be called a **program**.

P

An individual who is on the payroll of a nonprofit organization for the purpose of working on a particular project. The project may have been proposed to the organization by that individual and the hire made as a way for the individual to obtain nonprofit status for the project. The job may end when the project is finished, or the organization may opt to assign the individual to other projects. The degree of control the individual may have over the project depends on the agreement made when the nonprofit connection was made.

Proposal
See Grant proposal.

Query letter
See Letter of intent.

Questionnaire

A grant proposal format consisting of a list of questions indicating the exact information a foundation or government agency wants when a nonprofit organization is proposing a grant. It is similar to a regular grant proposal except that the questions become the headings for each section. The information in a boilerplate grant proposal can be used to answer the questions.

Request for proposal, (RFP)

An announcement issued by the government notifying the public of any new types of grants available to nonprofit organizations or individuals. The announcement describes the grant benefits and the application procedure.

Research grant

Funds awarded to aid a professional who has proposed a particular course of study. Research grants are often given to an institution, such as a hospital or a university, which in turn pays the recipient and research staff and furnishes the facilities needed for conducting the research.

Residency

A grant of working space plus room and board, often awarded to artists, writers, or musicians. Sometimes fees are charged for the accommodations, but usually they are lower than the market rate. The residency may be in a location that offers a collegial atmosphere with other recipients, or it may be part of a fellowship at a college or university.

Scholarship grant

A grant given to an individual to pay for undergraduate, graduate, or postgraduate education. Sometimes a scholarship grant may be distributed through an institution instead of being given directly to the individual. Graduate and postgraduate grants may also be known as **fellowships.**

Seed money

A grant or combination of grants given for the purpose of establishing a new nonprofit organization. These grants are not intended to fully fund the organization but simply to support the planning and start-up phase. They are also important in attracting additional grants, because potential donors like to know that other supporters are interested in an organization. May also be referred to as a **start-up grant.**

Sponsorship

A connection with a nonprofit organization made for the purpose of receiving a grant, in lieu of obtaining nonprofit status for one's own project or organization. It can be limited to a fiscal connection, or it may be more interactive, with aspects of the project shared with the sponsoring organization. Usually a contract spells out the details and limits of the arrangement. A fee may be charged by the organization to cover its services.

Startup grant
See **seed money.**

Statement of need

A section of a grant proposal explaining in a brief, general statement the problem that is meant to be remedied by the grant.

Tax-exempt

A status awarded by the Internal Revenue Service to organizations whose income is not subject to taxation. In the case of philanthropic organizations, all income is tax-exempt, whether it comes from gifts, sales, or other sources. The tax-exempt income can be used only for charitable causes.

Technical assistance

A type of in-kind donation popular with corporations, in which they allow technical experts on their payroll to work for a number of hours to benefit philanthropic causes.

Trustee

An individual who is a member of a board or managing committee that operates a nonprofit organization. If the organization is a foundation, the trustees may determine the distribution of its grants.

Volunteer

An individual who gives time and expertise without pay to help a philanthropic organization.

Welfare grant

A grant that is made available for people who are in need. Often welfare grants are offered in the aftermath of a catastrophe to those who have experienced injury or loss.

White paper
See **Grant proposal.**

index

X

Z

the author: up close

Barbara Loos learned about the importance of a strong mission statement and accurate financial documents as a reporter at *Fortune* magazine where she worked on various stories, including the "Fortune International 500." Since then she has worked as a volunteer for several nonprofit organizations and knows firsthand just how important getting a grant can be.

Barbara J. Morgan Publisher, Silver Lining Books

Barnes & Noble Basics
Barb Chintz Editorial Director
Leonard Vigliarolo Design Director

Barnes & Noble Basics *Getting a Grant*™
Lorraine Iannello Managing Editor
Matt Lake Editor
Emily Seese Editorial Assistant
Della R. Mancuso Production Manager

Silver Lining Books would like to thank the following consultants for their help in preparing this book:

Rebecca Balentine, Assistant Director Grant and Contract Administration, Yale University School of Medicine, New Haven, Connecticut; **Allison Chernow** and **Alexia Jurschak** of the Katonah Village Improvement Society, Katonah, New York; **Ann Rumage Fritschner,** a certified fund-raising and nonprofit consultant, Hendersonville, North Carolina; **Susan Caruso Green** of Fundraising Consultants, Cranford, New Jersey; **Caroline Harris,** development consultant, Gardiner, New York; **Paul Propson,** Director, the Michigan Neighborhood AmeriCorps Program, Ann Arbor, Michigan; **Steve Schaeffer,** a development director, New York, New York.

Photo Credits
Artville: 3, 12, 16, 20, 29, 42, 44, 48, 50, 56, 73, 95, 112, 121, 123, 125, 127, 129, 131-132, 138, 140, 146, 150, 156, 158, 160, 165, 173, 174, 176, 178; **Comstock:** 18, 21 (bottom); **Corbis:** Robert Llewellyn/Corbis 66, Mug Shots/Corbis 96; **digitalvision:** 1, 7, 25, 37, 63, 83, 105, 117, 137, 155, 169; **PhotoDisc:** 28, 30-31, 64, 68, 74, 130, 164; **PhotoDisc Collection/Getty Images:** 26, 106, 108; **Rubberball:** 76-77, 94, 118, 120